What's Wrong
(Unless You Think About It)

What's Wrong with Right Now?
(Unless You Think About It)

Talks with 'Sailor' Bob Adamson

Revised Edition

Editions INDIA
An imprint of
STONE HILL FOUNDATION PUBLISHING

EDITIONS INDIA
An imprint of STONE HILL FOUNDATION PUBLISHING
37/3352 Palliparambu Lane, Kaloor, Cochin 682 017, Kerala, India
editionsindia@asianetindia.com
stonehillfoundation@asianetindia.com

What's Wrong with Right Now?
(Unless You Think About It)

First published 2004 in the U.K. by Non-Duality Press
Revised by John Wheeler July 2004
This edition published 2009 by Stone Hill Foundation Publishing
Copyright © 2004, 2009 by Gilbert Schultz

ISBN 10: 81-89658-07-7
ISBN 13: 978-81-89658-07-6

Cover design: Girija Nair
Editing/copy editing: Girija and Mohan Nair
Proofreading: K. Meenakshi/Typesetting: Binu M.

Book composition by BookWorks STM, Cochin
Printed in India by The Ind-com Press, Chennai
Printed on acid-free, partially recycled paper
Distributed in South Asia by Stone Hill Foundation Media

For sale in the India, Pakistan, Bangladesh, Sri Lanka, Nepal, Bhutan, Myanmar, and Maldives only. The export of this edition outside these territories is prohibited.

Contents

Preface   vii
Introduction   ix

1. The Answer Is Not in the Mind   11
2. Are You the Mind?   35
3. Just As It Is   51
4. Presence–Awareness   67
5. Be What You Are   77
6. The Mind Cannot Change the Mind   91
7. No Thing   105
8. Open to This   109
9. Simply Know That You Are   123
10. Realise That   131

Testimonials   143

I am not speaking to any body,
I am not speaking to any mind.
I am speaking to that I AM that I AM,
to that Presence–Awareness that expresses
through the mind as the thought 'I Am'.
Just this and nothing else.

Preface

What you are in essence is self-shining, pure intelligence. The very idea of shining implies a movement. Movement is energy. So, I call it 'pure intelligence–energy'. It is shining through your eyes. You cannot say what it is, and you cannot negate it either. It is 'no thing'. It cannot be objectified. It ever expresses as that living, vibrant sense of presence, which translates through the mind as the thought 'I am'. The primary thought 'I am' is not the reality. It is the closest the mind or thought can ever get to reality, for reality to the mind is inconceivable. It is 'no thing'. Without the thought 'I am', is it stillness? Is it silence? Or is there a vibrancy about it, a livingness, a self-shining-ness? All these expressions are mental concepts or pointers towards it, but the bottom line is that you know that you are. You cannot negate that knowing—that you are. It is not a dead, empty, silent stillness. It is not about keeping the mind silent but seeing that what is prior to the mind is the very livingness itself. It is very subtle.

When you see that that is what you are, then the very subtleness expresses itself. That is the uncaused joy. Nisargadatta puts it beautifully. He puts it in the negative: 'There is nothing wrong any more'. We think that we have to attain something and then stay there. Realize that you have never left it at any time. It is effortless. You don't have to try or strive or grasp or hold. You are That.

Bob Adamson

Introduction

This is a revised edition of *What's Wrong with Right Now?* (*Unless You Think About It*). The first edition proved to be a turning point for many who read it. The clear pointers guide the attention back to the place where direct cognition is happening. The mind wanders about, so to speak, with the hope of gathering and accumulating some secret knowledge. Bob continuously shows the return journey, which is the elimination of erroneous beliefs. As these are cleared away, the clarity of simple, open awareness reveals its ever-present subtleness. It is with you now, even though you may feel it is covered over by a restless mind's activities.

This book can assist in bringing you back to the unchanging essence of what you are—the very first instant of being-ness, from which you have never departed. That is the peace that is beyond all understanding.

Gilbert Schultz
Editor

Chapter 1

The Answer Is Not in the Mind

There will never be any more God than there is now. Never more of good, wholeness, abundance, perfection, infinity than there is at this present moment.

*Living in this moment of IS-ness, the next moment unfolds as a continuity of Grace.**

Bob: There is never any other time than right now.

Question: Can time exist?

It is always presence. When you are thinking about it, it is presently. Time is a mental concept.

Q: Who wrote this text?

In the context that it was written, it does not matter who wrote it.

Q: How and why did the One become many?

In non-duality, in one-without-a-second—not even the One, just pure presence–awareness—how can the experience know itself? It is complete; it is whole; it is perfect. To re-experience that, it puts a veil of ignorance over itself, as it vibrates into different patterns with experiences and expressions through these different patterns. Then it turns around and comes to know itself again, returning to its completeness. The Hindu tradition calls it the dance of Shiva, the play of God, *lila*, or the sport of God.

---

* From a text given to be read by those present at the meeting.

So, in reality, nothing has ever happened. Patterns of energy appear. It is still the same intelligence–energy. Patterns appear just the same as the reflections appear in the mirror. What has happened to the mirror?

Q: Nothing! Is there mind or are there several minds?

There can only be one mind, if there is any such thing as mind. Mind is an appearance also! So it can appear as many.

Q: Do I know myself through the mind, or is it independent of the mind?

The only instrument we have is the mind. So, it has to be understood that you can never grasp it with the mind. Because it contains the mind; the mind can never contain it.

Q: What about the feeling or the thought 'I am'?

That is the primary thought from which all dualism appears. As soon as there is 'I am', there must be 'you' or 'the other'. That idea 'I am' is the cause of all our seeming problems. That sense of presence is expressing itself through the mind, but prior to that thought, you know that you *are*, don't you? You are not thinking 'I am' constantly all the time, are you? You know that you are sitting there. You are aware of being present, continually.

Q: What about when I am in deep sleep? I am not aware.

The mind is in abeyance in deep sleep, but that effortless functioning is still going on. The mind is not there. That functioning is still breathing you. It is still causing the blood to flow around through the body. The fingernails continue to grow. All these do not stop because the mind is not there.

Consciousness, or the mind, stirs in that deep sleep, and you start to dream before you are awake. In this dream you create a world, and you see yourself taking an active part in it. It might be in a town, a city, a room or out in the country. You can dream of all sorts of things. There can be other people there. There could be cars, animals or anything, and you see yourself taking an active part. Yet, that body has not moved from the bed. All of this seeming world has been taking place in that little space between your ears. If you continued to dream every night and the dream continued on from the night before just as it appears to do in the waking state, could you tell the difference between the dream state and the waking state?

So, is the world anything other than mind? What substance has the mind? What substance has a thought got? That 'I am' thought is what you believe yourself to be. Can the mind stand on its own? If you were not conscious, if that consciousness was not there, could you have a single thought?

Q: *I don't know!*

Well, you just said that even in deep sleep you were not aware of it. No thoughts. The mind is dependent on consciousness or awareness or whatever you want to call it, that pure intelligence–energy. So, that must be primary, that must be the reality, not the 'I am' thought, not the 'me' as such.

Q: *Is consciousness dependent on anything else?*

That is also just a movement in awareness. All this world appears in that consciousness. All this world is the content of consciousness. So, it cannot be anything other than consciousness. There is nothing that you can think of, conceive of, perceive or postulate outside of consciousness. Even if you are talking about other universes or other solar systems, the moment you think about or talk about them, you have brought them into consciousness. When that 'thinking and talking' consciousness is out of the road, there is that pure intelligence there. It just shines of itself.

Q: So is consciousness a part of the universal?

The whole thing is the universal, if you look at it closely. No parts. Awareness, the absolute, consciousness, mind are one and the same thing in different aspects. As with water: you have water vapour or steam, then the liquid state of water, and then there is ice. These are three different aspects of the one thing—water. So, it still never changes from that non-dual one-without-a-second. Grasp that fact and stay with that. It does not matter what appears. It is still only the One. Then that sense of separation can no longer be there.

Q: How do we account for the population increase then? If all is one and nothing can be taken away or nothing can be added, how do we explain the population increase?

Well, it can vibrate into myriads and myriads of patterns.

Q: Does that imply that something else is losing?

No. What is the something else? It is still that one and the same intelligence–energy! They say that this universe as we know it started off as an atom or a quark or something minute. All this energy started from that. From our point of view, it is still expanding, and that original so-called beginning was fifteen billion light years ago.

In a drop of water there are myriad forms of life. Within that life there is more life on a finer scale. Going out into space, to where the Earth is just a speck, that is another, quite different point of reference. Now, where is it all judged from? It is still all within that One. To get a true judgment of it, you would have to step outside of it. That is impossible!

The time-scale differences between the life in the drop of water, the life as we experience it and the life out there in deep space are vastly different. The life of a cell could not possibly conceive of our life of a hundred years. It is all relative to the reference point taken. Our reference point is always that 'me' or 'I', but added to it are events or experiences of what happened yesterday or last week or last year or when I was born. These are added to that pure 'I' image. It has built this image that I am a good person or a bad person or I have low self-esteem or I am angry or fearful.

That very sense of 'I' is separation. That very sense of that separation is insecurity. From being the totality, the unlimited potential of being, we have immediately become an isolated, separate human being with all its limitations. We have built this mental cage around ourselves. Now, from that reference point (which is based on 'yesterday', the past) everything is judged.

You see that whatever has happened to me is judged from that reference point and I might consider it 'good' or 'bad'. Our criteria, our reference point, is never correct, never true. In seeing that, in grasping that, where does it leave you? It can only leave you right here, right now, aware in the actuality of this moment. This is the real! *This* is the real! *This* is the real! *This* is the real!

Q: So, we are whole, complete—nothing to need but just a thought away from being insecure and neurotic.

Yes. If there is no thought, what is wrong with right now, if you're not thinking about it! If everything is just as it is—unaltered, unmodified, uncorrected—what is it? It is just as it is! Just one, as is!

Q: It puts your dreams in a different perspective. They are real!

Yes, they are very real while you are dreaming them. But when you wake up in the morning and see them as a dream, what happens?

Q: I guess, basically, you dismiss them, but sometimes I try to get something from them.

Well, do you carry them around all day and say, 'That was terrible?' Trying to get something from them would be perpetuating the 'me' or the self-centre that thinks it is going to find an answer.

Q: In the dream, it seems so real, it seems that it actually happened.

It seems so very real, but when it is seen as a dream, you are no longer bound by it. Just the same as when you see the falseness of that self-centre, that it has no reality either, then you are no longer bound by that and that is the freedom. That is freedom from the *seeming* 'bondage of self'.

Q: I am just thinking that my past experiences are useful if the need arises.

Your memory is there to be used. It is useful. But when memory comes up and carries on and carries on, it starts to use you. It will make you fearful, anxious, or depressed, or whatever. It is using that self-image that you have of yourself. If that memory is not good for it, then 'I don't want to be like this' pops up. So you create another image in the future when you are going to escape from all of this.

As we said before, the mind is the only instrument that we have. The mind is not the enemy just because it causes all the problems. If it is understood clearly, then it is there for what it is meant to be there for. It is a wonderfully creative instrument. But when it believes that it is running the show, then the trouble arises.

The mind is so closely aligned with that pure intelligence–energy. And because it has never been questioned, it has come to believe that it is the power: 'I am me', 'I am running the show!' But when you look at it closely, you see that all it is, is an image, an idea, and on its own it cannot do anything. It actually relies on that pure intelligence–energy.

Now, right now, you are hearing and seeing. Does the hearing say, 'I hear'? Does the seeing say, 'I see'? What says those things?

Q: The mind!

So, in saying those things, the mind has given itself the power, believing that 'I am doing something'. Let's look further. Does the thought 'I see'—does that see? Does the thought 'I hear'—does that hear? So, that is the proof that it has no power. But you're still seeing. You're still hearing. Effortlessly, the functioning, the happening, is going on. Effortlessly, that pure intelligence–energy is bubbling up through this psychosomatic apparatus, this body–mind, this pattern of energy. You see that all the activities are happening.

Q: So, I just have to learn to trust in that.

It is not a matter of trust. It is just coming back and seeing that there is no 'me' to trust. You see that the 'me' is only an accumulation of ideas in your mind, an image based on your past and your conditioning.

That pure 'I am' thought is one move away from reality. And because that is pretty hard to grasp on its own, it has added all these other images and ideas and words to it. This has created an image, which seems very real and solid because it has been gone over day after day, week after week, from the time we were two years old. It has never been questioned. And that is the only problem. Once it is looked at, the false cannot stand up to the investigation.

That 'I', that 'me'—that thought can't see. It can't be aware. It can't breathe you. It can't beat your heart. It relies on that pure functioning for the thinking itself! Yet it has come to believe that it has the power.

Without thought, do you ever stop being?

Q: Intellectually, I understand completely everything you have said. If I said (again language is a barrier) I want to know what I know intellectually as direct experience, what can you do for me?

Right now, you're hearing?

Q: Yes.

You're seeing?

Q: Yes.

Feeling?

Q: Yes.

That is direct experience! Is thinking happening?

Q: Yes.

Do you hear that tram going by?

Q: Yes.

You know immediately it is a tram before it comes into your mind as thought. That is pure intelligence registering everything just as it is. A split second later you say, 'That is a tram' or 'Someone coughed' or 'Someone moved'. At that point you have stepped off the razor's edge. Prior to that is the pure registering of everything just as it is. The pure intelligence of itself does not change. It does not move. It is just like the mirror; it reflects everything just as it is. The difference with the analogy of the mirror is that the mirror has to have stuff outside of it.

Like the sun, that pure intelligence shines of itself. All this vibration, this movement of energy, is registered just as it is. The mind comes in with discrimination. It has preference, partiality or comparison. It is the nature of the mind to divide. It is the nature of this manifestation to be in the pairs of opposites. Could there be silence without sound? Could there be stillness without movement? What can you compare them to, without the opposites? Looking at it from this perspective, there is no big bad ogre in all these pairs of opposites. They are understood for what they are.

So, your direct experiencing is right here, right now, presently. It is always direct experiencing. Full stop!

(*Pause*)

The mind is starting to move away from it with, 'What if such and such', isn't it? Hearing! Seeing! Feeling! Living! Breathing! Immediate! It is Immediate! You will notice that that is always first and foremost. It is only the habit of the mind to latch on and seemingly take you away from it. But when is that happening? Isn't it presently? You can only be thinking presently. If you are thinking about the past, you must be thinking about it presently. Thinking about the future, you must be thinking about it presently. You have never moved away from it. It is only seemingly that you do.

A little bit of alert awareness, seeing what is actually happening, then are you going to be 'bound' by it? No. Because you have seen the falseness of it. It is not going to stop you going into the past or the future, but you understand it. You have seen through the illusion.

Q: So how does the Jnani (sage) function?

The same as anybody else. Functioning happens. But he knows that there is no personal doership because it is seen clearly that there cannot possibly be a person. The idea of a person is an erroneous belief, a belief in that sense of separation, the 'me'.

When you see that there is no 'me', you must know for certain also that there is no 'other'. I know that there is no centre here (*indicating himself*), and I know that there is no centre there (*indicating the questioner*). So then, who is superior? Who is inferior? What is there to be afraid of? Who do I need to hate or resent?

Q: If there is no centre, how can you have consciousness?

Consciousness is all there is. There is no one to *have* consciousness. The whole thing *is* consciousness.

Q: In my conscious mind I'll have the intellectual awareness that there is no separation, and I will experience the experience with this awareness. Is that the best that the mind can do?

You are breathing now. You're seeing, hearing. It is all happening. Now, is there any need for a 'me' to allow that to happen?

Q: No.

But it is seemingly so, isn't it?

Q: As soon as you come into thought, it appears to be so.

Yes, but when you understand that it is only appearance, is it going to change?

Q: No, I wouldn't think so.

You see, you understand that the sky is not blue. Sky is only space. And when you get up in a plane at thirty-thousand feet with space all around you, it is still clear and empty, the blue is always further out. We have believed it to be blue, but when you understand that it is *not* blue, you will still see it as the same blueness. But you know full well the truth about it. (That is another thing that Christ said: 'Know the truth and the truth will set you free'—that you are not that separate entity!)

Now, it experiences and expresses itself through all this diversity. A dog has the characteristics of a dog. A cat has the characteristics of a cat. So-called human beings have characteristics with the functioning of a human being, with their mind and body, etc. But knowing full well that you are not that, it is not going to make any difference to the functioning. It is still going to happen. As the Zen text says, 'Before enlightenment, chop wood, carry water. After enlightenment, chop wood, carry water'. Before, it is a chore that is happening for the 'me' that might like it or might not. Afterwards, it is just part of the functioning, part of the happening.

Q: But the nature of the thought affects the activity of the world.

Exactly.

Q: This means that your life and what happens depends on your awareness.

Yes, in other words, you're being lived.

Q: So, theoretically, I could walk across Port Phillip Bay and even calm a storm.

Yes, exactly! That same energy that is contained in that atom, which this universe as we know it came from. How many atoms are in that body? Look at the potential energy that is there. Now, what stops that? We think, 'I am a separate human being'. We put the block on it. The block is the word.

Q: So, it is not a matter of bringing truth or the One to this level of consciousness? To say that this level of consciousness can't live as One because it is contained in the One. ... It is the illusion of separation.

Yes, but you are particularising the consciousness. It is one universal consciousness. That is a trap also. You are being lived, so what would you do? Get as much of the blockage and the idea of separation out of the road and let the living-ness happen. That is 'taking the brakes off'.

Q: How do you get out of the road? That is like the person trying to do that, isn't it?

Yes, that is right. That is badly put, to say to get yourself out of the road. You just see the falseness and continue to see it. Look, investigate and you see the falseness of the so-called person.

Q: Yes, I feel like it's the person looking, the person trying to see that there is no person.

What happens is, first off, all there is is the seeing. Take that chair over there as an example. The thought comes up, 'I see the chair'. There may be some association with the chair, which I don't like. The colour is wrong or whatever. So, the psychological response to the seeing is 'I like it' or 'I don't like it' or whatever. That response is the 'me' or the self-centre. So, the seeing has then been split into the seer, this image that I have that doesn't like the chair. The chair, which is named from memory, becomes the seen or the object. Prior to that, in the immediacy, is just a registration in which there is this seeing. This seeing contains the chair and the response also. But the psychological response is the 'me', with all its likes and dislikes. Its prejudice and partiality is all that the person is.

If I am aware of that just the same as I am aware of the chair, then what has happened? In that awareness is just the seeing because it is seeing not only the pseudo object but the pseudo subject also. If it is taken on board as 'I am seeing it', then the pseudo subject, believing that it has the power or the reality, is seeing an object. That is all that ever happens—objectivity.

The first object you see is the front of this (your) body. But we don't take that to be an object. We take that to be the subject.

Q: What is it that stops an instant transformation when I hear this? Why can I hear about this and it doesn't impact? Is it because I am hearing through the mind that filters it or is it just not time?

None of it 'rang a bell' as we say?

Q: Oh yeah.

When it is recognised—and is not just taken on an intellectual basis—it is recognised to be true, and then that is yours from then on. It may not come up for a day or a week. But at some particular time it will come up in your livingness and you'll say, 'Ah! That's what that is'. And you will know it in your own understanding. It may be the same words or different words altogether. With the knowing of it, the recognition of it and the understanding of it, then it is grasped. This will continually go on.

If you can do the same with what I have been saying about the self-centre—seeing the falseness of it, that it is only an image, that it has no substance—then that strips it right away. The mind will continue to think in the way that it always has. As long as you are embodied, you're going to have that mind. It is still going to think in the same way. It can't think in any other way than in the pairs of opposites. In understanding it, you are no longer bound by it. The old habit patterns will come and catch you for a while, but they have lost their intensity, and the further you go along, the less they bother you.

Q: Is it correct to say the following? For the appearance of movement—the physical movement of the energy that we observe—for that movement to appear, there must be something that is rock-hard solid for it to appear on?

It is not rock-hard solid. It is just like the reflecting surface of the mirror. Like the sun shining in the sky—now can the sun know darkness? No. If it can't know darkness, can it know light? No! Yet it shines of itself. Its nature is to shine. Now, the nature that is emanating from that body–mind organism—it is shining through your eyes; it is hearing through your ears. It is that same intelligence–energy. Its nature is to shine. We put the clouded mind upon it and become poor depressed, anxious souls.

So, allow that essence within you to shine. Let it shine through your eyes and light your eyes up. Let it permeate your whole physical being with its healing essences. It was there before the brain was even formed. It is vibrating and pulsating through you now. It is one and the same energy.

It is that 'all presence'.
Q: How do I get to it? I know I am already it; how do I perceive it through the mind?

Just see the falseness of the 'I'. Then you are left with it.

Q: I can understand that, but it is not happening. Can you make it happen right now?

It is happening right now! You're hearing. You're seeing. The functioning is going on as pure experience right now. The trouble arises because you are looking for something to grasp with the mind and say, 'This is it!' You see, you are looking for an experience in the mind to say 'Ah! That's it'. And then all you do is tuck that away in your memory, and you go along on your merry way looking for something else.

When they say in the *Gita*, 'The fire can't burn it; the water can't drown it; the wind can't dry it; and the sword can't cut it', what does that mean? Why can't the sword cut it? Because it contains all of those things, including the sword. Now, you will never find the answer in the mind. It contains the mind. The mind can never contain it. As we pointed out earlier, before that thought 'I am' comes on to you, are you aware?

Q: Yes.

Right! That's it! But you can't say anything about it! That doesn't sound right to the mind because the mind is looking for some experience. It is very subtle.

Q: Why can't I stay with that?

When do you move away from it?

Q: When the mind comes in.

When is that happening?
Q: What do you mean?

When the mind comes in, isn't it presently?

Q: Yes.

Well, you are still with it. You are only seemingly moving away from it. What past is there unless you think about it?

Q: Yes, there is none.

There is just now! So, you see that past is an idea or an image in your mind of a moment ago or last week or yesterday, but it is happening presently. You only imagine that you have moved away from now. The same with your anticipating and imagining tomorrow or a moment away.

Q: How do I stop this imagining?

It is not necessary to stop it if you understand what is happening, if you understand that it is still presence. When is it happening? Just ask yourself that question. When is all this happening? The obvious answer is that it can only be happening presently. So, is it anything other than presence? The happening itself is movement of energy. Thoughts are subtle sound. Sound is energy, and energy is just vibration. So, it is that omnipotence, that 'all-power'. It is omnipresence; it is 'all-presence'. And the knowing of that, the awareness of it, knowing that I am, the pure knowing, is the 'all-knowing', the omniscience. It does not mean to know this or know that; it is just pure knowing. Pure knowing is the totality of knowing.

Are you not that right now? Aware of being present? In the Hindu terminology it is *sat-chit-ananda,* or being–awareness–loving. You are aware of being present. And you love to be. Full stop.

You are aware of being present. Anything else is still

happening presently. Just the focus needs to move back a little bit and see. Instead of focusing on what we have been used to focusing on 'in the head', just pause for a minute and see the difference between that pure intelligence, the registering of everything and the thinking about it. Realise that you're hearing those cars go by while you're listening to me, probably with your full attention. You are still hearing and seeing other things, and it is still being registered. Try listening in here—in here.

The first seeing is formless. In that formlessness there are still forms appearing out there. The first hearing is silence. But there is still hearing out there. You are that formless, silent, pure being. It is very subtle. Stay with it! To the mind this is very boring: 'Oh gee! I can't live in silence and stillness!'

Q: It is almost too simple for my mind to grasp.

Exactly! Let the mind go. It is that simple, so simple that we miss it. It is pure simplicity itself. Stay with that subtleness, that silence and stillness, and you will see things and understand the ancients when they talk about 'The peace that passes all understanding'. It cannot be understood by the mind. There is no peace of mind. It is the nature of the mind to chatter. You are not that chatter. The mind oscillates between the pairs of opposites. Peace is where the mind is not.

Q: Is there any way to stop this chatter?

No. Do you chatter? Understand and watch it. If you haven't got a vested interest in it, what is going to happen? It is going to die down. You see, when the chatter starts and I attribute it to 'me' and 'I want this' or 'I don't like that' or 'He said so and so' and 'blah, blah, blah, blah'—I have a vested interest in it. Now, in that vested interest what is happening? The energy of 'I' and 'this'. The 'I' is a thought, and the 'this' is a thought. But that energy is opposed to itself. It is a dissipating energy. It is in conflict with itself. But if I understand that there is no centre here and that it is just chatter and I am aware of it, then there is no 'me' that wants anything out of it. There is nothing resisting it. It is just what is. Then there is no energy going into it.

Now, can a thing live without energy? No! So, in the watching of it, in the awareness of it without bothering about it, in seeing it for what it is, that it is false, it is going to die down of its own accord. So, there is no need to try to stop it. In trying to stop it, the mind will be in conflict with the mind. That will get you into all sorts of trouble, which it has done until now.

Q: How do we stop? I see that chatter but I am still giving it value.

Well, keep watching it and ask yourself, who is this 'me' that is giving it value? Until it comes up and you see that this 'me' is only an idea. Where is this centre? Where does this so-called me start? Look and try to find a centre or a spot in your body that you believe is 'me', or in your mind that you believe is 'me'. Look as hard as you like. If you can find it, you come and tell me! I know for certain that there is no particular place in this body or this mind of which I can say 'This is where I begin', 'This is where it all starts'.

In your own looking you will find that the false cannot stand up to investigation. You are not the hand; you are not your ear; you are not your nose. There is no particular spot where you can say 'This is where I began'. Have a look at the body. It started off as a single sperm and a single ovum, which were the essences of the food that your mother and father ate. Where is that cell? That would be the centre, that would be the start of it all, but that cell has doubled and redoubled, and it is long gone.

From another angle, am I this mind? The mind is just composed of thought. Which particular thought am I? Am I this 'I' thought, but where is that 'I' thought if I am deeply asleep or unconscious? It is not there! That would be the finish of me if I was that 'I' thought. But the breathing is still happening; the functioning is still happening; there is no centre there.

So, when the chatter goes on and you see that there is no centre to attribute it to, then it must lose its hold. It becomes laughable.

Q: So, even if there is no chatter, in this consciousness, one is living and being. One consciously knows that one is an expression of the One, and it is an illusion of duality that is creating an experience for the One to know itself …

No. If you say it's a delusion, you're putting the separation on it. If it is just what is, you can't say anything about it at all.

Q: What my consciousness says is that I don't experience it on levels that I know other people do experience it. I heard a well-known Swami talk a number of years ago, and he said that with yoga practices, with meditation practices, one gets to know the mind, to use the mind to go beyond the mind. It seems to me that consciousness cannot know anything outside of consciousness. That seems to be the dilemma. Our interaction here is on the level of consciousness. So, wouldn't it be the technique to learn how to 'be still and know that I am God'? Wouldn't meditation practices be the best you could do to get there, if there is somewhere to get to?

Whatever this Swami or anybody experienced, it is still not it. The so-called transcendental states are still not it. It does not matter whether there is silence here or chatter because both to me are still experiences. But that pure knowing, which they both appear in, that pure registration of everything, that is beyond experience. That is pure experiencing.

If it is understood with the mind that no matter what experience appears can never be it, that the answer is not in the mind, then you are not concerned with wanting to experience some so-called ultimate state or non-state. You just stay with the subtleness of 'being now' and see what is in that. See what appears from that, the uncaused joy, the uncaused happiness and the pure compassion that comes up. As soon as they are expressed through the mind, that is the name that you give them, but you cannot say 'I am experiencing this'.

Q: No, the Swami said that it was necessary not to be a prisoner of the mind. But he talked about techniques then—to become more aware of the mind, to start to know the nature of the mind.

There are all sorts of techniques; I can give you some techniques if you want them. If you can grasp what has been said here and take it away with you, it is going to hatch. It is going to bear fruit.

Q: Yes, well, that is what I experience. To know something on an intellectual level is one thing, and I relate to what you said about starting to own something and then it starts to become your truth and then you change. That is a process I am familiar with.

Well, then you know because it has already happened to you. That is why you are familiar with it. So, it will happen again. It has brought you from other places to here. Despite ourselves, it takes you where you have got to go. Not that you have ever been anywhere!
   (*To a regular visitor*) How is it all sitting with you?

Q: These two are saying exactly the opposite. They say that intellectually they know but they don't experience it. I would rather say that you are experiencing it right now but intellectually you don't know. Does that make sense?

Yes, that is well put. Intellectually, you don't recognise that you are the experiencing itself.

Q: Yes, and that's it. There is nothing to know. The mind keeps on wanting to know, wanting to know. It is causing a problem by wanting to know.

Exactly! And when you understand that no matter how far you go, the answer is not in the mind, what would you do? Full stop. I am not going to bother looking there anymore.

Q: But I do keep looking there.

Yes, because that is habit. It is understandable because we have been conditioned from an early age, day in, day out. Just like the smoker reaches for a cigarette whether he is thinking about it or not. The habit is there. But in seeing it for what it is, the habit is starting to be broken.

Q: So, if a newborn is in the company of say someone like you, would it also continue on like us or would it know instantly?

Well, it soon takes on the conditioning of the world. The young child is often laughing and doing things spontaneously and quite naturally. But after a while, at about the age of two, they learn to scowl, to stamp a foot, and you see the conditioning starting to form. Then they go off to school where they learn different looks, putting on little tantrums. And so it goes on.

Q: That can't be stopped?

No.

Q: You can really only know the world through the mind, through the word?

Yes, but know it for what it is and there is no problem.

Q: But you have to experience it to know it, don't you?

Yes. You're continually experiencing it. But just know it for what it is. You find that things just happen. You just sail through it. You see so many people on the tram or bus or train, locked in their heads, their eyes down. They are not looking around at the trees or traffic or the others on the tram. It becomes almost palpable.

Q: It is like your own little private prison.

Exactly! The bondage of self. The cage we have built around ourselves, made by words.

Q: We are very fortunate to come across this other view.

Well, if it happens that way for this so-called particular human being. What brought you here?

Q: What do you think it is that brings us?

It is that same consciousness, that same essence, that so-called, particular entity returning back to its own completeness. It has experienced itself and expressed itself in its ignorance. Now it has got the joy of coming home.

Q: What I understood about twelve months ago, with prayer and meditation, where you allow the light to come in, you break away from that self enough to allow something to come in, to break that sense of bondage ... I know with my experience, I got to the point where I was not going to live anymore. Something had to give.
  We are talking about the bondage of self. I know that the bondage of self kills. I have lived the life of addiction, so I know that. So what is it? I know what it is for me, but what is it that draws people? I always believed that it was because someone prayed for me. But I don't know what I believe now.

Love is another term for light. Christ says, 'I am the light of the world'. That is that 'I am', that sense of presence. By what light do you see the world?

Q: Through the energy, I guess.

Exactly. So light or love is that energy expressing through that body–mind organism as that light. That light has sort of pierced the cloud. From the so-called point of view of that body–mind entity that is so clouded over, it could not grasp it within its own orbit. So, it manufactures something else, like the Fellowship for instance. Then it will bring you to someone who 'knows'. The whole essence is functioning, and it puts in your way what is necessary to bring you in a full circle. It might be a person, a book and—bang!—it starts you on your way home.

Q: I was in the Fellowship for twelve years and I had no concept of a higher power. I was the ego and it 'ran amock', and then suddenly I had a spiritual experience just come upon me.

It took that time. At that particular time the openness or a letting go was there or the self was out of the way, and the fruit had ripened at that particular point. Not all fruit ripen at the same time. Some may never ripen.

Q: Could you quicken the process?

We told you before that you are already there!

Q: I am going around in circles.

Well! Full stop!

(*Pause*)
Did you stop? Stop thinking? Hear the bird singing? Are you thinking about that? It is happening! It just is! The conditioning, as we have just said, is that the mind wants to know. The mind, in wanting to know, will perpetuate itself. It will go down every direction it can find. So, whichever direction you go in, you're still in the mind!

There is only one way to get out of that: full stop! In that instant of stopping, there is clarity; there is just what is. Just a second later it starts up again. But if you see it in that instant, the instance will widen. In the registration of what is, just as it is, right here, right now—without any modification, alteration or correction—that is what is. What could modify it, alter it or correct it? Only the mind, only a thought or feeling.

If I ask you, 'What is wrong with right now, without thinking about it?', what would you say? You have to pause for a moment and realise that if there is no thought there, there is nothing wrong. In that instance you have also stopped it. That is it. That is where it is. That may seemingly be only instantaneous at the moment. But if that sinks in often enough—that there is nothing wrong unless I am thinking about it—then even if the thinking is going on, you know that you don't have to take any delivery of the thinking. That is the cause of all my problems.

In that split second without that thinking I still existed. I still was! Focus more with that. The mind is not the be-all and end-all that we have believed it to be. Believing that we can't live without it or can't exist without it, we have placed so much importance on it. See that it is not so important. Though it is a wonderful creative instrument, but it is not so important. The livingness is going on effortlessly, right now.

Go along those lines. Investigate yourself and see. It will hit you: 'That's right!' It (the mind) is not so important. Then it starts to lose its hold. You will never be the same again. Whenever you get the chance throughout the day, question. Stop and see: 'What is wrong with right now if I don't think about it?' Is the 'I' seeing? Is the 'I' aware? Or is the 'me' seeing? Is the 'me' aware? Or does the eye say 'I see' and does the ear say 'I hear'? Realise that the functioning is happening effortlessly without any 'me' involved.

It is only the thought 'I' that comes up and says 'I see'. But the thought cannot see! So you see what an erroneous thing the mind is telling you. In seeing that, you can never believe it again. If it tells you erroneous things in that respect, then it must have told you a lot of other erroneous things. It told me that I needed to drink at one stage. It had me believing it so much that I became obsessed with it and

I didn't think I could live without it. For many years it had me believing that I needed to smoke. When it was really questioned and looked into, I needed neither of those.

The mind can tell you erroneous things because the reference point is a dead reference point. It is based on yesterday. Question it continually and see whether it is telling you correctly or whether it is based on some past dead image. Do that for a little while, and you will see. Those beliefs won't be given any credence anymore. Yet, when the mind is utilized, it is a wonderfully creative instrument.

Chapter 2

Are You the Mind?

As you all know, we talk about non-duality here. The only reality you are absolutely certain of is the fact of your own being. First, we would suggest that you just relax. Don't try to grasp what is being said necessarily with the mind. Because, as you see—or as you will see—the mind is the problem. Just relax and be receptive, because the words that are coming out here presently are coming from that intelligence–energy.

If the mind is not acting as the cloud (as an obstruction), what will be receiving those words is that same intelligence–energy. Then what is apperceived or grasped or understood will come up through the mind at the appropriate time, which will be presently, at the appropriate place, which will be here and now. Then the appropriate activity will take place from that. So, that is what we suggest happens here.

No one—right here, right now—can negate his or her own being-ness. Each one of us knows that 'I am'. That 'I am' is not much to hold on to, if it is just purely and simply 'I am'. So it adds to itself all the events, experiences and conditioning, and forms an image, an idea. This idea or image is believed to be what I really am. All our problems arise from that.

That is so because the very idea of 'me' separates 'me' from 'other than me' or 'non-me'. Separation is isolation; it is loneliness; it is fear; it is insecurity; it is vulnerability. This is what we continually do. We separate, and we continually search for wholeness or security or happiness. It is not our fault, it is not our parents' fault. It is the way we have been conditioned, the way they were conditioned.

If I believe that I am separate, an individual, a separate entity and person, then I am insecure. So at the first level, the family level, I try to have a warm and loving family around me to make me feel secure. Then, there is the tribal level. And if I can be 'in with the tribe', then I will be more secure. Then, there is the nation. And nations go to war with nations over that same self-centredness or insecurity— divisions and separations.

And yet all the great scriptures, all the great religions, all the great traditions will tell you that God (if you like to use that term) is one-without-a-second. It is non-dual. It is just this present awareness, just this and nothing else.

Some of the Christian scriptures will tell you 'I am the Lord thy God; there is none other'. Another term they use is that God is omnipresence, omniscience and omnipotence. It is all-presence and all-knowing and all-power. And they mean exactly that: non-dual, one-without-a-second, presence–awareness.

Now, where does that leave room for a 'you' or a 'me' or anything else? If there is a 'you' and a 'me' in this all-power, all-presence and all-knowing, that means that it is not all-knowing, it is not all-presence and it is not all-power. So, from that point of view, all of this manifestation can be nothing other than That. And that is one of the great sayings from the Hindu tradition: 'Thou Art That'. Because there is nothing other than That. 'I Am That' is another great saying.

Is there anyone here right now that is not that presence? You are present, right here and right now. Is it your presence? Is it my presence? Is it each one of us as individual presence? Or is it all-presence? Is there anyone here that is not knowing that right now? Is it your knowing? Is it my knowing? Or is it somebody else's knowing? Or is it omniscience, all-knowing? Knowing implies an activity, and all activity is energy. You hear the cars going by; you hear the other sounds in the room; you see the movements in the room. All sound, all movement, is it yours? Is it mine? Or is it somebody else's activity or energy or power? Or is it omnipotence, all-power?

Just have a look at this and see it clearly. Then ask yourself, 'Who am I?' What is this 'I' or 'me' that thinks itself to be separate? Where does it start? Where does it finish? What is it? You see the search, as I said previously, is always going on 'out there'. 'Out there' is where we have been conditioned to look, gathering something that will make me secure, that will make me whole, that will make me happy.

If it is not in the family, the tribe or the nation, then it is in a better job, more money, better relationships, a good house, all sorts of things out there. The belief is that the more I accumulate, the more secure I will be. Or, if I go on some spiritual search, I will become realised or enlightened or whole and complete—all anticipated to happen in some future time.

I can go on all through my life doing that. If it doesn't look like it is happening in this lifetime, then what do I do? If I am a Christian, I conceptualise a God somewhere who has a heaven somewhere in the future. If I am not doing too well 'here' and I say my prayers and do a few good deeds, I will finish up 'there' at some future time. All that is, is conceptualisation!—an idea of some future time, of some future place and some future deity or being that will make it right for me. Or if I belong to an Eastern religion, I will reincarnate—at some future time! I will have another life, never realising that there is only now! Never looking to see what it is that is going to have this other life, to see what it is that has got 'this life' or seemingly thinks it has got this life.

It is quite simple. If you look, you will see it quite clearly and easily. What does this body consist of? The essence of food. Where does the food come from? It comes from the earth, and the earth from the fire. Fire, water, air and space—it is nothing but the elements. Where do the elements come from? Well, in that vibration, that movement, these things appear. And so they are nothing other than energy, that one energy (omnipotence). The mind is the same thing. What is the mind? The mind is nothing but thought! Thought is subtle sound. Word is sound. What is sound? Vibration. What is vibration? Energy!—Omnipotence again, appearing as different.

So, I have never ever moved away from it. I have never ever separated from it. So, it is foolish for me to try to seek wholeness, completeness or whatever at some future time. I can look at the mind again and ask myself, 'What past is there, unless I think about it? What future is there, unless I think about it?' In looking at that, I can see clearly that there is no past and there is no future unless it is thought.

I can bring yesterday's events—from my memory—into my mind right now. But they are not the actual. For instance, I met 'so and so' yesterday, spoke to him and shook his hand, etc. Well, is it the same today? I may have forgotten some small details and added some that weren't there. So, I have made up this present concept or idea of what went on. Or, I anticipate or imagine the future. I imagine something in the future, which I can get fearful about or ecstatic about. But look closely. When is all this taking place? Isn't it taking place presently? Can there be any other time that it takes place in? You can say, 'Oh yes! It took place yesterday'. But when are you saying that? Isn't it presently? Or you can say tomorrow is going to be a different day. When are you saying and thinking that? Isn't it presently? Now, it is all happening in that presence. Is it any different from that presence, that omnipresence, all-presence?

You can say all is God. Wrong! God is all! All is only an illusion. All is not. 'All' is only a word. A word is not the real. It has never been real. 'Water, water, water'—you can't drink the word 'water'.

These words—these words!—are nothing, in the same way. But isn't there omnipotence, that vibration, that movement of energy? Is it going on here? There? Or anywhere in particular? You can feel it. The hearing of the word—right now—is a vibration. That which is hearing it is vibrating and pulsating. The heart is beating, the lungs are expanding and contracting. Feel the energy moving around in that body. Is anyone not knowing that they *are*? The omnipotence is functioning. When is it all happening? Presently. And omnipresence is functioning.

Seeing this, understanding this, I can see how I have

been caught. I can see how I have put a seeming limitation upon myself. I put a cage around myself that does not exist. Have you seen a bird in a cage that has been there for many, many years? You can open the door of that cage, and the bird is not going to fly out straight away. You can leave the door open for days but the bird will not take that step to fly out of it.

We point out here and continually point out the cage. But we say that even the cage is a phantom, it is a false idea. It does not exist. How many of us step into our freedom by hearing that? It can be done, right here, right now. The understanding is that you have never been bound, even though it may seem that you have been.

What is the limitation that I place upon myself? First and foremost, it is this idea of being a separate entity, a 'me'. How does that come about? Purely and simply, if I look at the mind and see how it functions, then I see that, being a movement of energy, it is a vibration. Being a vibration, it can only function in the pairs of opposites, which is the past (memory) or the future (anticipation and imagination). And in that range it can still only function in the pairs of opposites. If it is not happy, it is sad, or pleasant/painful, loving/hating, good/bad, positive/negative and so on. It is still functioning in the pairs of opposites. And what is it using? Words! Purely and simply words.

Often, when things happen, we say, 'It doesn't matter'. And when you mean it and it doesn't matter, nothing comes of it. But if you take some thought or idea aboard and it does matter, that is exactly what it does. It matters and becomes concrete. We beat ourselves over the head with a word. We punish ourselves for the word.

Call something anxiety. Show me some anxiety. Show me some fear. That word becomes very real when it is allowed to dance around and vibrate in the mind. What does it refer to? It refers to a reference point, the 'me', which has felt this feeling before. And it has named it 'fear'. And so, as soon as that thought or whatever it is, is seen, immediately comes up the old response from the past, which it refers to, the reference point or the centre. The centre does not like it. It doesn't want to be here. It wants to escape. So, it immediately resists it and gets into conflict by trying to force it out, change it or do something with it.

So, this word that has no power of its own (because it has got no substance, it can't stand by itself), has now caused the blood pressure to rise, the goose pimples to rise on the skin, the hair to stand on end or whatever. So, you see what 'fear' (or any other word) can do. But if I am not taking that word on board, if I am seeing it for what it is, have understood that the word can never be the real, it is just let go of! It appears presently. It is witnessed presently. The response is witnessed. Nothing further. Full stop! Nothing further happens with it. The response is not entered into—not trying to change it, not resisting it, just seeing it for what it is: it is a word. So what happens? You see, that energy hasn't taken off; it hasn't started.

Once the energy has started and builds up, then what is it going to do? The action must follow.

Ever wondered how a cyclone starts? It is only energy blowing the air around. It builds up and builds up, and look at the damage it can do. You have seen the storm clouds in the sky with the lightning and thunder. It builds up and builds up and—bang!—down comes the rain. It is all released. Nature does not carry it around like we do. We get a thought or an idea, and the continuity of thought becomes feeling and emotion. It is gone over and over and built on and built on continually. Look at the damage it does to the physical body. Look how seemingly real that cage becomes: 'Poor me, I have got no self-esteem' or 'I have low self-esteem'. And it begins to show in the physical form. I walk around with my head down and my shoulders hunched. You look at somebody and wonder what they are thinking of you or what they are going to do or not do: 'This or that is going to happen' or 'How am I going to survive in the world?'

What has done all this? Purely and simply, all it is, is a word—a simple vibration, a vibration that has become a cyclone, a tornado within us. It rips us apart. But when has it all happened? Has there ever been any other time or any other place than right here, right now, presently? Has it ever moved away from that all-presence, that omnipresence?

So, the word—as I said before—or the body or the mind or any of this matter is nothing. Presence is that which appears as matter. I can't move away from that presence. There is nobody to move away. Any movement, any vibration, anything that is happening, it is that omnipotence appearing as something other, appearing as matter, the shape, the form, or as the name we put on it.

Right here, right now, nobody yet has negated their being-ness or that sense of presence. Is there anything wrong with that, unless you think about it? When I do think something about it, what is thinking? Can the thought think itself? Or does thinking appear on that presence, on that awareness? Is it anything other than presence, seemingly appearing as different?

Is there any need for any conflict? Is there any need for any dissipation of energy? When you look at the mind and see that the reference point doesn't like this, or wants more of this or whatever, 'this I don't like' is just an idea or a bunch of words I have. And what it likes or doesn't like is another set of words. It has a name for it. If it doesn't like it, it is trying to escape from it. If it does like it, then it wants more of it. So, there again there is a struggle to acquire more. That energy is seemingly fighting with itself just through wrong understanding.

All you have to do is look at nature again, and you will see the opposites at work in nature. They are there: day and night, tides coming in and tides going out, seasons coming and going. You will notice one thing in nature, and that is that the opposites are not in opposition to each other. The incoming tide is not fighting with the outgoing tide. Winter is not fighting with summer. Look at your own body. The incoming breath is not struggling with the outgoing breath. Your heart is not in conflict with the expansion. It doesn't get halfway in expansion and suddenly say 'I am going to contract'. It is only in the mind that this conflict goes on! The only reason that it goes on in the mind is the idea of that separate entity, the 'me'. When that is seen—that there is no separate entity—then who is there to get in conflict with anything? Things will come, things will go. That awareness, the alertness, the appropriate activity, takes place spontaneously and intuitively. It is still going to happen in the pairs of opposites: it might not be good at this moment; it might be bad, or something other. If the conflict is not there, it will resolve itself quickly and effortlessly. It may not be the way that 'me' and memory wants it to be. But I only have to look back over my life and see many things—most of them—not the way that this 'me' of memory ever wanted them to be! Not the way that this 'me' thought they would work out or wanted them to work out. Most of my life it has been like that. Most of the struggle was because this 'me' wanted to change it.

All of the conflict was caused by 'me', and looking back over my life now I see how, through all the dramas and traumas, how beautifully it all fitted in. I see how it has all fallen into place for this so-called entity at this particular spot at this particular time, without that so-called 'chatter in the mind' today. It doesn't mean to say that the chatter doesn't go on. But the chatter has no fire any more. There may be lots of silence here—and there was a time when I looked for silence and peace—but that was also just another experience. It does not matter; it is not allowed to 'matter'.

That is so because there is that understanding and knowing that, that which all of this has appeared on—that omniscience that it is—has never been touched by any of that. Nothing has ever come near it. If we must put words to it, it is that still, silent, blissful being-ness. All words, which are not the real!

But remember what we said at the start. Never mind the words. Just hear and feel the resonance in the word, the vibration, the energy. Is it any different from the hearing? Sense and be aware of the vibration where the hearing is taking place. That knowingness, that awareness, is still appearing presently. Has it ever changed?

Are there any questions?

Q: What do you think of meditation in terms of what you said on the chatter in the mind? How do you deal with the chit-chat of mind and the going beyond that chit-chat?

If there is awareness, that it is all taking place presently, when are you ever out of meditation?

Q: In terms of getting to that stage ...

When are you saying this?

Q: Well, I am saying ...

When are you saying this?

Q: We are talking in the 'now'.

You're saying it presently. So, where are you going to get to? You see? You see what you have done? The mind has taken you to some time in the future. This is what we constantly do.

Q: OK. Yet, I still feel that discipline and aspect of working towards something on an everyday basis. Because we still need to live lives on a practical everyday basis.

What do you think I do?

Q: So, I am talking about ... how do you actually implement this awareness in an everyday life in practical terms? And I would say that meditation is a way of connecting and strengthening.

When you say meditation, *who* is going to connect with it and *who* is going to implement it in their daily life?

Q: I would say myself.

So, you're saying 'me'. So, what is this 'me' that is going to do it? We pointed out earlier that the 'me' is only an image, an idea.

Q: I would say that I tend to be dualistic at times. I recognise that about myself. So ...

Is that you?

Q: The dualistic aspect?

Yes. Have a look at the world. The world is dualistic. If it wasn't in this material manifestation, you would not know that there is a world. That is how it appears. But you say that you tend to be dualistic. Is that you?

Q: Well, it is kind of my experience in this living process.

Who is the 'me' that is experiencing it? You see what I am trying to get at? To bring you back to that original awareness, so that you don't continually jump out into this seeming entity that you have created. If you ask yourself this question, 'Who is this happening to?', what would the answer be?

Q: It is a projection of myself.

Of 'me', yes, but who is the 'me' that this is happening to? Where is this centre? Where is this reference point that you are referring all this to?

Q: Well, it is a 'separated me'.

Yes, but where is it?

Q: I don't quite understand the question.

Where is the centre that you are referring to? The separated 'me', where is it? What part of it is you? Where in your body or your mind is the self-centre that you are referring to?

Q: *It is in my mind.*

Exactly! In your mind. Now, are you the mind?

Q: *No, but I can't deny the mind does exist in the manifested state.*

Yes, but you are not the mind.

Q: *I am beyond the mind.*

All right. Now you asked the question, 'How do you function in the world?' Now, if you are beyond the mind, you must be aware of what is happening in the mind! See?

Q: *Yes.*

So, what appears in the mind, what goes on and the activity that follows on, is that you?

Q: *At times it is, unfortunately!* (Laughs)

What I say is discard this 'I' that can't say that 'I am beyond the mind'. If you say that you are beyond the mind, that that is your actuality, then function from that point. The mind is appearing on that, on that pure intelligence that you are. But what it is judged from is by the mind itself, an image you have of the past. Now, being aware of that, are you going to lock into anything in particular? If something happens that this reference point 'Jane' doesn't like, you are going to do something about it. You're immediately there, and you have got to try to change it. But if that reference point is only mind or word—it is not your reality—what are you going to do about it?

Q: *Leave it alone!*

Exactly! If the energy is not going into a thing, can it live without energy? No. So, it will disappear! Where did it come from in the first place? Where do any thoughts come from?

Q: I would say that that is what meditation really is. It's really working into that very origin of being and learning to work with the mind in terms of it becoming a servant to that higher entity.

But when you meditate, what do you do?

Q: It is still a practice for me. I sit quietly and become aware of a silence and the sounds moving in and out of the silence. And gradually I feel that the energy is lifted and raised in the body until the vibration gets very high.

Yes, but you say sit quietly. Who has got this idea that 'I am going to sit quietly'? You get the idea? You say 'I am going to sit quietly and meditate'. So, that is the image again, the idea to sit down. And we try to still the mind or we try to watch the thoughts. So, that is the 'me' or the reference point.

Q: I would say that it is more or less coming from a reference point in terms of the higher connection.

What is a 'higher connection' or what is a 'lower connection'?

Q: It is where the mind does not come into play and influence. It is beyond the mind.

Did you hear that tram go by just then?

Q: Well, it passed through …

Yes, that was registered on that pure intelligence, just as it is, right at this moment, just the same as all the other sounds. You're hearing; you're seeing; you're tasting, touching and smelling. These are all registered just as they are! Now, until I drew your attention to that, the mind did not think a thing about it. But it heard it pass through.

So, that pure intelligence is registering everything just as it is. That is meditation! Meditation is when you are never away from it. But when you think 'I am going to meditate' or 'I am going to quiet the mind to get a higher connection', that is where the meditators are using the mind to try to quiet the mind. You can forcibly still it for half an hour, and then what goes on? It races away and gets caught in the same rubbish that it was in before!

Q: Do you think so?

I know so! I am talking from experience. But when there is nobody here, who is to meditate, what is there to meditate on? That doesn't leave you a blank. It leaves you totally alert in the moment, totally aware! Where you are not only aware of everything around you, you're aware of what is happening in the mind also, first and foremost.

Are you aware of your thoughts?

Q: Well, I am not consciously concentrating on them.

No, but you're aware of thinking?

Q: Yes.

Right. You're aware of those trams going past again?

Q: Yes.

They are objects. You are aware of your thought, and your thought is an object also. So, take it from that viewpoint, that they are both objective. Who is the subject? It is That which they are all registering on immediately, that pure intelligence. That, the mind cannot grasp. Why? Because it contains the mind. So, it is pointless trying to get at it with the mind. Only see the mind and understand the mind.

Then you will realise that you are already there. The registration on that pure intelligence is functioning right now, presently, in its fullness, as it has always done. Have you ever moved away from that?

Q: No. I forget about it!

You forget about it! When do you forget about it? Wouldn't it be presently?

Q: Yes.

So what is it? It is still only presence. All the forgetfulness is still only presence. You have never moved away from presence. The mind is not you. You, that omnipresence, is the mind! Even when you are forgetting about it, it is still there.

Q: Yes, words.

That is the bondage. That is what we have trapped ourselves in. And the word is not the real.

Q: Thank you.

So, what will you do now?

Q: Well, I will take my own journey. In terms of us intellectualising and talking about it and the actual living of it and experiencing it—that is where I feel that certain practices are helpful.

What I was pointing out to you was a direct experience. You see that and come back to that and you continually see that. That is continually your direct experience. You are not 'Jane' experiencing this or experiencing that. It is just pure experience. It is happening continually. Then the mind interprets this or that experience immediately after the event. That interpretation is only from the dualistic point of view of the mind—which this manifestation is. But to see that it is pure experience and the functioning is happening, to see that 'Jane', as such, has no reality as that seeming person, then the spontaneous functioning happens through that thing which we call 'Jane'. You see that, that is what always happens.

If you see that there is no centre now, when did you ever have a centre? You never did, did you? If there is no centre now, then there could never have possibly been one. So, that means that you have never had any personal volition. The life, the functioning, has gone on; even though you thought you were running it, the functioning has happened.

From that point of view, when you understand that, instead of trying to run it and change it or alter it, you go with the flow of it and allow it to happen much freer than what was apparently happening before, with the seeming 'me' putting the 'blockers' and 'stoppers' on.

Q: OK. How does one perhaps remain true to that aspect when we go about our daily lives, when we are using the mind in terms of functioning, and then it plays some tricks on us and becomes our master rather than a servant? In practical terms, how do we work with that aspect of ourselves?

If there is alertness there, if that awareness is acutely alert, then when the tricks start to come up, you see them.

You say 'using the mind'. That is what the mind is there for, to be used. It is not the enemy, though it is the cause of all our problems. If it is understood, then it is wonderfully creative. All the art, architecture, technology, all the teaching of yoga, and whatever you are doing is coming through your mind. It is only when it is in conflict with the 'me' and the 'other', and seemingly in that separation, that it causes us pain and suffering. You get trapped in that habit pattern. And that is all it is, because over the years you have been conditioned to that way of thinking and believing. It has become habitual. Seeing the habit of it, you don't fall into the trap of it. You might get trapped for a while because that habit pattern is seemingly strong. But if you have seen the falseness of it all, it can never be as intense as it was before. And eventually, it won't even bother to come up because the energy won't go into it. It will be seen. There will be an awareness of it as soon as it starts.

Chapter 3
Just As It Is

The description can never be the described. All we are doing is describing what is. Right here, right now, presently, is what is happening. There is nothing other.

Primarily there is that registering of everything. Just like that mirror on the wall is reflecting everything in front of it, so that essence, intelligence, or whatever name you like to call it, is registering everything just as it is. You heard that siren, but you didn't have to say it was a siren. You are hearing this voice, seeing the sights in the room, feeling your body sitting in the chair—all just as it is. And—just as it is—what can you say about it? You can't say anything at all about it. From that point of view, it either is or is not. The description can never be the described, the 'what is'.

The thinking is being registered, also. That is discriminated into 'this thought' or 'my thought' or whatever the word might be. Rather, be aware that it all is just as it is.

Say you are walking somewhere, and you are not naming anything; there is no thinking going on. You are passing houses, trees, picket fences, or whatever is in the street. Everything is registering immediately. You don't have to name each individual thing. Your thoughts might be happening, and your mind might be totally involved in those thoughts. Yet one piece of concrete paver may be higher than the other, but you won't trip over it. It will be registered immediately, and the appropriate steps will be taken over it.

Or if there is a crowd walking in the street, you're not going to bump into everyone. You find yourself avoiding people quite effortlessly without having to think, 'I have to dodge around this one'. Yet they will be coming from all directions and all places, but that intelligence is registering everything just as it is. And in the moment, the proper activity takes place.

It is the same with thoughts, also. As you are going along, you're passing this house or the next house. And as you are going along, thoughts are happening, too. They are registered just as is. What happens? The house you have just passed has disappeared from view or the picket fence you passed is gone. Thought is registered just as is, also. What has happened to that thought? It is left behind. It also disappears. One thought might be acted upon, the next may not be.

The only way we can change what is, is to correct it, modify it, or alter it in some way or form. The only thing that can do that is the mind: 'The chair over there is in the wrong position, and I want to move it'. It is no longer what is. It is what I think I would like it to be. That is all that has happened—the thinking 'That should not be there'. That thought, of itself, has no power whatsoever. It is only a thought; it is only based on words. But it refers to this 'I' that I believe, or have believed, myself to be up until investigation. That is so because what has been added to that 'I', that belief, has become the 'self-centre' or the 'reference point'. Everything is evaluated from that reference point. And because it is closely associated with that pure intelligence, it has come to believe, also, that it is the intelligence.

Like the piece of iron in the fire, it will get red-hot and burn, just like fire. Now, if the iron had a mind, it would think it was the fire: 'I am going to burn this and that'. But take it out of the fire, and what can it do? So it is with the thoughts: 'I can', 'I will', 'I am'. Take them away from awareness or consciousness or that pure intelligence; what substance have they got? Can they stand without that? Can you have a single thought if you are not conscious or not aware?

Constantly over the years, with the habit patterns going on it, (thought) has believed itself to be the intelligence. It believes it has reality, it has power, it has will; it can do what it likes and what it thinks it wants to do.

That is why this investigation is needed. Just stop and question. Have a look at what we have believed ourselves to be. Thought can't of itself do anything! Because that thought 'I see', can't see! The thought 'I hear', can't hear! The thought 'I am aware', can't be aware! But there is seeing, there is hearing, and there is awareness. It is happening right now!

The seeing itself cannot conceptualise. It cannot say 'I am seeing this'. Neither can the hearing say 'I am hearing this'. It is just pure seeing and pure hearing. It is conceptualised by the mind, which must refer to some past memory to get that name. The mind or the 'me', the thought that I have about myself, is the past. That is all it is. It is the past, and the past is dead. It is gone. It has happened. It is not what is. That centre we constantly refer to or believe in is a dead image.

Now, can you understand why the centre can never be happy, it can never be complete or whole? Because it can't keep up with what is. What is, is this manifestation, this transient manifestation, which is constantly changing. Like the river, it is constantly flowing. How can a bucket of water, taken from the river, keep up with the river? It is impossible.

So, we tell you right here that what you are seeking you already are! The idea of a separation is only a concept. With that idea of separation, there immediately comes along with it the sense of insecurity and vulnerability. Anything that thinks or believes it is separate must also feel isolated and alone, apart from 'me', other than 'me'. That is the way the mind functions. As soon as there is 'me', there must be 'other than me', and that is the seeming separation. That is the cause of all of our problems. When that is understood, what problem is there, if there is no centre to refer it to? Got it?

Q: The mind is just thinking that there is a problem.

Exactly. It is the nature of the mind to start stories and add to them and keep adding to them. You must see from that, that there can never be any answer in the mind. So, if there is no answer in the mind, what must happen? Whatever direction you go in must be in the mind. So, full stop.

In seeing and being with that, even in that split second, to know that there is nothing wrong with right now unless I am thinking about it, then, after that, does it matter whether the mind is there or not? Because if the mind has been seen through and understood, it is not going to be granted the same belief, just the same as in the understanding that the blue sky is not really blue. But we still see it as blue and acknowledge it when saying, 'What a beautiful blue sky!' But we know the truth about it.

As the scripture says: 'Know the truth, and the truth will set you free'. Know the truth about yourself! You will see that you ever were free. You were always free. Just a seemingly erroneous belief: we ignore our true nature and believe in the appearance.

Q: You have got to use the mind to reach this conclusion, but the mind has such deep programming. The idea of intellectually knowing the truth ... I find in practice I can know it, and I can try to stop the mind but, basically, it takes time for me to accept it gradually. I can be told it. I can understand it a little bit more and a little bit more. It takes time.

As you say, we have got to use the mind. Well, the only instrument that we have is the mind. That is why the mind needs to be understood—understood thoroughly! Then it is there as a very useful instrument.

You say that all this programming is there. Now understand: the mind is the past; it is the 'me'; it is the conditioning, all this so-called programming. Can the mind be rid of this past?

Q: I would have thought it was more about putting the mind in its place.

Yes but can it be rid of the past?

Q: No!

No, of course it can't because it is the past! When you see that, what would you do?

Q: Well, I would say I would stand back from it.

Exactly. So, what has happened to the past if you are not involved with it in the mind?

Q: Well, it is just a part of the mind.

So, what has happened to your programming?

Q: It has gone.

Right! That's it, purely and simply.

Q: Yes, but the technique would have to be constant.

See what you are doing? You are starting up another story instead of staying with it and seeing it for yourself. In seeing it, you won't be worrying about techniques. To have a technique means that you have to use the mind.

Q: The technique is to stay with it, to stop. But I call it a technique because I have got to say that I will make a decision that whenever I am aware that my mind is doing anything, I stop—stop and say 'Who am I?' or whatever.

It won't have to do even that! You know that the answer is not in the mind, that the mind is the past. You have stopped long enough to see that at one time or another. Then, does it matter whether the programming goes on? What is the programming then? Who does it belong to? It is *seemingly* happening. Is it going to have the same intensity that it had before?

Q: The operative word for me is 'knowing' it. What I have found is that eventually they become my truth. I know them, and there is no problem. I know them. But at the moment, this mind keeps going, and I use techniques to control this mind, to the extent that I focus on things and do some work.

Who is the controller? If there is a seeming control going on—who?

Q: I would say that decisions are taken.

Of course, decisions are taken. What is this 'I' that is saying it? It is happening in this moment. It is happening presently. You are aware of that going on. Now, if that 'I' thought can't see, can't be aware, has no power of its own, then when did it ever have it?

Q: Well, it never did.

That means that all the seeming decisions you have made, all the activities that you have ever done in your life, have not been done by you as a separate entity. That is what has happened.

Q: Yes, I don't have a problem with that.

So, any control that has come up, anything that you have said that you have done, has happened in spite of the 'you' being there. Anything you have thought, felt, tasted, touched or smelled is happening effortlessly, just as your breathing is happening effortlessly. Your heart is beating, your hair is growing, your food is digesting—all effortlessly without a personal doer. The thing is that, because you believe, and have believed for so long, in personal doership, you take on personal responsibility.

Q: So, you're saying that you walk down the street, and you get to the corner, and you don't know whether to turn right and go down and get a newspaper or go left and do something else. You stand at the corner, and the mind says, 'What will I do? Will I get the newspaper or will I go and have a cup of tea? I think I will get a newspaper'. Now, as I see it, that mind has done a job.

Yes. It is there as an instrument to be used.

Q: Even though there is no 'I' making decisions, the mind still has to make decisions. So, the mind has to say 'Do this or that' and so on, or 'create this or that or don't'.

The mind, when it sees that it has no power of its own, aligns itself with that intelligence. It is a receiver for what comes from that intelligence. The problem arises because it translates that input as this particular thought and 'I will do' or 'I won't do'. Without its being put into the idea of a 'me' (which is the past and has lost the spontaneity of the moment and is referring to yesterday), without that, it is functioning directly and spontaneously from the intelligence.

Q: In our tradition it says that 'the spiritual path is all-inclusive, never exclusive'. It is an incredible statement. So, everything that is possible for me to experience is it! I am a done deal because I have no say in the matter.

When it dawns on you, you realise 'Ah! I realise it'. If it is one-without-a-second, it is non-dual. Nothing is excluded.

Q: What I find is that there is an incremental freedom. Sections keep falling away. I know intellectually what you are saying, but as far as the lights going on, no. They just fall away bit by bit.

There is a wanting of some experience to be able to say 'This is it'.

Q: Is it possible to have a deeper understanding?

Who would have a deeper understanding?

Q: So, if it is not possible to have a deeper understanding, it is not possible for anyone to know what a dead mind would feel, sound, or look like?

What is a dead mind? What mind is there? What is the mind? Apart from thought, is there any such thing? The mind is the 'me'; it is the ego, it is the past. It is all of those things. When that is seen, it is dead—right then. When that is understood, what more is necessary? That is why Nisargadatta said, 'Understanding is all'.

Q: I am dealing with people's traumas all day. It is a constant contact with trauma for about eight hours a day. Afterwards, I go home to a young family and experience the growing children. It is an incredible contrast. Although mostly I feel relaxed and detached from it all, I do find myself being swept away by all that. I still find myself feeling deflated or sorry for myself. I still suffer constantly.

Where would all this be happening in those others that you see?

Q: Well, there are genuine physical symptoms, but most of it is in their minds.

So, what is being referred to is the image they have of themselves—that is the cause. And the effects that are coming up are from that. But when you understand that the image you have has no power, are you going to fall into the same old hypnotism, the same old conditioning? Or are you going to step away from it?

Q: I still fall into the trap of analysing 'why' or 'where' that is coming from.

Get back to the basics. Everything is registered right now, just as it is. The only thing that can change what is—alter it, modify it or correct it—is what comes up in the mind. Now, that content in the mind is also registered just as is.

What happens? You leave it there. You don't try to carry on modifying or correcting the thought that has come up. But this is what we do: 'I don't like this' or 'I shouldn't be doing it' or 'I shouldn't be thinking'. It is still as is. And what is wrong with right now, unless you're thinking about it? What is wrong with right now if we are thinking about it and not locking into the thought, if we are just seeing the thought for what it is? It is also just what is! Then it loses its sting.

But first see that it is the 'I' thought that is the cause of the seeming separation. See that it is the cause of all our seeming problems. It becomes the reference point for everything. Everything is relative to 'me'. It is good, bad, pleasant, or painful according to what the 'me' thinks about it or what idea it has about it. See that the thought is not the real thing. Then, how can you ever believe in it again? The word itself is not the real thing. It is only pointing at something.

Q: I know now what we are talking about. But the mind has this perception that it is a prisoner, that it is separate. And there is pain because of that. But, intellectually, no. It is a thought. On an emotional level, I don't accept it.

What is the emotional level? What is the difference between the thought and the emotion?

Q: The mind creates the emotions.

Yes. So, they are on the same level. You are not accepting it with the mind because, if you see clearly now, can that mind see? Can it be aware? Can it think? Can that thought 'I see', see?

Q: No, no.

Are you seeing right now?

Q: Yes.

See that without the thought that seeing is happening, hearing is happening. You don't need that thought to see, to be aware.

Q: I am allowing myself to have these thoughts to discuss this with you. But I am not troubled because I don't allow them.

But see what I am getting at. If the 'I see' can't see and the 'I hear' can't hear, what do you attribute the intellectual level and the other level to?

Q: Yes, what is that? That is one, there is no separateness.

Well, there can't be two levels. The intellectual level must be contributing to the 'I see' and 'I hear' as being different from the pure seeing and the pure hearing. What is the primary truth that is with you right now?

Q: I suppose it is 'I am'.

Yes, knowing that *you are*! That is not some thing! That is just pure knowing. That is not intellectual. There is no need for the mind for that! So, to know something, there is a concept in the mind. You see, you are hearing those cars go by; you are seeing the colours in the room. What is happening? There is an immediate knowing of that. You do not say 'That car is going by' while you are listening to me. It is registered. And that means there is a knowingness of it. It is not intellectual. That is the difference between the thinking mind and that pure intelligence. It is a very subtle split.

Can't you see that there has to be the knowing first? Then it is labelled by the mind.

Q: I do know it, but this mind says 'I don't know it'. This mind keeps creating its own reality.

But it can't! It has no power. If you see that, then you won't believe it anymore.

Q: No, well, I don't believe it.

If you don't believe it, if it is not believed in, would there be any energy going into it?

Q: No. I don't think so.

No. It has come to a stop then. It can't live without energy. The reason it is going on is because you are still continually feeding it. You are believing that it has some power. You are not seeing that, of itself, it can't do anything.

Q: Whenever I become aware of ...

That is involvement with the mind! There is no becoming. You *are* aware! Come back to the primary. Can you have a single thought without that awareness? Awareness is there already. Can you fall out of presence?

Q: No.

No. Whatever is going on is nothing other than presence. But you are giving it name and appearance and believing in the name and form, giving it that seeming reality by the belief in it. Belief becomes the reference point then.

Q: I don't have a problem with any of that. What I suppose we are talking about here is the ultimate truth.

You are that! You have never moved away from that. Whatever appears on it is nothing other than it, appearing as different. Where can you go?

Q: Nowhere.

Right. Even with all those words you use, you haven't escaped from it.

Q: Yes, I think this word 'realised' is a good one, to become re-alised!

There is no becoming! What you are, you already are.

Q: I don't have a problem; this mind that is communicating with you doesn't have a problem with all these concepts and this truth. But ...

Never mind the 'but'. If you don't have a problem, then leave it at that. Full stop. And you are there! See what I mean? That is the subtleness of it. The mind wants to create another story. If you're not creating another story, then you have got to be quiet. The last concept you have to drop is that 'Some day, I'm going to get it'. What time is there?

Q: Yeah, now!

Right. Full stop! Drop the concept of having some future time that it is going to happen in, and there is no problem.

Q: This 'Who am I?' is a beautiful thing. You don't get an answer. All I experience are those three words that are not a question. I am just one with those three words.

When you ask the question 'Who am I?', look for the source or even where that question came from. Can you point at that source? Is there any particular spot in this body or in the so-called mind where that question arose?

Q: No.

Any place it disappeared in?

Q: No.

So, what are you left with?

Q: Nothing!

Nothing, not a thing. That is definite proof that all this re-ferral to a 'me' or a centre has no particular place where it begins and no particular place where it ends.

Q: Yes, I agree. I see that there is no difference between the pre-state, where all the talking and thinking occurs, and the state of just talking. There is no difference.

There couldn't be any difference, could there? Because it is one-without-a-second. It is omnipresence; it is all-presence. That includes all the conversations, all the feelings, all the thoughts, all the manifestation, the whole lot. It is omni-science; it is all-knowing. It is knowing the intellect. It is pure knowing.

Q: So, one is incapable of being deeper than another because of that. I sit and argue with these people who say there is a fathom-less, bottomless depth to this thing that exists 'before the talking'. I just react to that. Then they say that that reaction is a belief in a self-centre. What does that mean?

A belief is another reference point or a centre. Why do peo-ple rise up in arms when you attack their beliefs? Because it questions their centre. That is what they are referring to. If they are Christians or Buddhists and 'This is *my* belief', they immediately get all up on end. Because the sense of seeming security is in that belief.

That is why I say that it does not matter if there is silence here (and there can be long periods of silence), or it does not matter if the chatter is going on seemingly non-stop. They are both experiences. They are both appearing on that pure knowing. The mirror will reflect the so-called 'good thing' and the 'bad thing'. It doesn't make a scrap of difference what it is. It is just as it is. So, everything is reflected just as it is. Even the discriminating processes that come up with that are still reflected just as is.

Q: So, the ongoing things like jobs and parents and children—that is just the ongoing energy and consequence and conditioning and all that.

If the focus is not on all that chatter that goes on about it, then it is going to appear effortlessly. It will fall into place, whichever way it goes, just like your breathing or your heart beating.

Q: So all this suffering comes from the competition, the jostling one-upmanship?

Have a look at it. As soon as that 'me' is there, that is the primary separation. The mind functions in the pairs of opposites. It cannot function any other way. So, as soon as there is a 'me', that implies that there is something 'other than me'. So, if I am not whole or complete, then immediate insecurity comes up. All that jostling is about trying to gather as much around itself as it can, to get as strong as it can, to seemingly protect itself.

But if you understand what the scriptures tell us, that it is that one-without-a-second, omnipresence, omniscience, that presence, then you see and know that everything is that. You have never moved away from it. In knowing that, there is total security. Know that you are birthless, deathless, timeless, spaceless, bodiless and mindless. The happenings go on, but to *whom*?

Q: Yes, but the mind wants a win.

Yes. But seeing that the answer is never in the mind, you know that you can't win. So drop it! Why bother with it?

It will dawn on you. Just like when you walk out of the house and you get a mile down the road and it dawns on you that you have left the keys at home. It will just dawn on you. Why did you leave your keys at home? Just a little bit of inattentiveness to what is, at the time. It will just dawn on you.

We have been conditioned to look 'out there' for it. We have been looking in the wrong direction. When you turn back and ask 'Who am I' and find that there is no 'me'—the 'me' can't see, can't hear, can't be aware—then when were you ever separate? The whole thing collapses. It collapses immediately. If there is no separation, where can I go? What can I do? Can I ever get away from it? Can anyone ever fall out of presence? Even when you say 'I have forgotten', when are you saying it? You're saying it presently! The very act of saying it is presence.

Q: What about when the mind gets into illusion, like fear and such?

You see, as soon as what *is* is named as fear, immediately there comes that belief of pain. And there is an immediate movement trying to escape it. If it just is what is, do you have to move away from it? You are seeing it fresh and new. Could it be fear?

Q: That is the hardest thing! Any kind of understanding is being an individual. But not being an individual, you are everything! You can't win ever, being an individual.

When you go to 'Who am I?', you can't find where that thought starts because there is no particular place where it starts, where it ends. You cannot place it anywhere inside this body. So, it means it is everywhere and nowhere. The mirage is still going to appear. But when it comes up after that, if that is seen, you know it for what it is. You have seen through it. It is still there. It is still seemingly real. It is just like the blue sky: you will still acknowledge it by saying, 'What a beautiful blue sky!'. But you know full well that it isn't blue.

So, the 'me' comes up, just like the actor on the stage. You're acting it out. Things are happening. But you know damn well that it is not what you are. Nothing has changed, yet everything has changed.

Q: Well, what has been happening is this. When I hear you say that the answer is not in the mind, I see that the answer is in the present moment.

You have the answer immediately—a realisation. If the answer is not in the mind, where else can it be? It must be right here, right now, as what is. So, you know the answer. And that is pure knowing.

Q: Until that dawning happens, you're constantly bringing that intellectual understanding into the present and trying to get that imprisoned mind to experience the awakening. It is incredible that when we hear that the answer is not in the mind we don't just go there.

You can't go there, and you can't get away either!

Q: But from the point of view of the mind it is something that it wants to get.

It is all right here, right now, as what is. In knowing that, how can there be any conflict? Relax and be what you are.

Chapter 4
Presence–Awareness

Q: There is an idea that is currently common in the bodywork modalities that all of the tissues have some sort of memory. If you stimulate this part, then there may come up some emotion, or memories are triggered.

Instead of going back or trying to look back at it, start from the source. What is it? It is all energy, isn't it? Every cell is pure intelligence–energy, and in the space between the cells is pure intelligence–energy. So that energy has to flow. The body is a pattern of energy, and the mind also is a pattern of energy. They are nothing other than that.

The nature of the mind, which is vibrating as this pattern of energy, seems to divide everything into the pairs of opposites: good/bad, pleasure/pain, future/past or whatever. And these thought patterns, what are they? The energy in the mind is the same energy that is in the body. We say it is connected, but it is one and the same thing.

A lot of the memories from the past get locked in the body. So, the energy is blocked. When there is a realising or a seeing of some of these things, then that energy is released, and it starts to flow again. It might come out as thought patterns or memories or pain. You see it clearly and you think, 'Well I've released that'. But it never really had any substance. It is just the energy that is seemingly blocked there and stagnated. So when one is expanded and open, the energy is flowing. There is no problem.

Q: But if there is tension or a headache, what does one do?

Come back to the source and ask, 'Who is it happening to?' Thoughts are coming and going, and the energy is vibrating right now. Then there is nowhere in the head or the body where it can lodge.

But all this is a sense of belief. We give it some sense of reality, of realness, of concreteness. And so our beliefs are a problem. If you haven't got that belief, if you're not taking a stand anywhere, then there can be no seeming blockage, can there? What the blockage is, is energy resisting energy. If I don't like this (what is happening), then the resistance comes up, trying to alter or modify what is. Why do we try to alter, modify or correct what is? Because we believe we can do it better or 'It shouldn't be like this'. That is all based on our previous conditioning. If that wasn't there, it would be as it is anyway, wouldn't it?

In one of the old Chinese scriptures it says, 'In the mind, no mind. In the thought, no thought'. A lot of people mis-interpret that. It doesn't say don't have thought. What it means is to have the thought 'no mind' in the mind and the thought 'no thought' as a thought. With that thought 'no thought', the thoughts have no chance to take hold. Benoit said, 'When a thought appears, just step over it'. Then another thought will come, but you're not fixating on anything. They just come and go. Then there is no chance for any tension to lodge anywhere because it is not abiding anywhere.

We all say 'I am'. That sense of presence expresses through the mind as that thought 'I am'. Now, that sense of presence, is it your sense of presence? Is it my awareness of presence? Or is it just that sense of presence? This pure present awareness, just this; there is nothing other than that. So, if you are seeking illumination, realisation or oneness with God or whatever, then let it be seen directly that what you are seeking, you already are. You are already and always have been.

You see, you might like to call it God (or whatever concepts you want to put on it). I prefer to call it intelligence–energy. A definition of God is omnipotence, omnipresence and omniscience. That means all-power, all-presence and all-knowing. Where does that leave room for 'you' or for 'me' or anything other than that? So, any concept about 'my' God being better than 'your' God or 'my' higher power or lower power is nonsense. Where is there room for you, if God is all-power and all-presence?

This is what we point out here directly. That there is just that one-without-a-second. This intelligence–energy is expressing itself effortlessly. Your only problem is when that sense of presence is expressed through the mind as the thought 'I am'. Conditioning has been added to that thought 'I am' and it has formed an image. At about the age of two years, reasoning started to happen to you, along with events and experiences. And this has formed an image which we call 'me'. It is an idea, a thought in the mind.

Now, being mechanical, the mind can only function in the inter-related opposites. This thought 'I am' is what has caused our seeming separation. It is the primary dualism: I/not-I, self/other. As soon as there is an 'I', there must be a 'you' or a 'this' or 'that' as opposed to 'I'. And so, with that 'I' and 'you', there is an immediate sense of separation, an immediate sense of fragmentation, which is isolation, lone-liness, fear and insecurity. If I believe that I am separate, then, quite naturally, there is that insecurity there. There is that seeming sense of isolation and fragmentation.

From then on our life is geared to becoming whole, happy, complete. Because the conditioning is 'to look out there', we seek it 'out there'. As it was said earlier, first, we seek a secure, loving family around us. The next level is the tribe. Then the next is the national. Nations go to war with nations to try to protect that sense of insecurity, that vulner-ability which we all have. We are frightened that something or someone will take something from us.

We have to add and accumulate as much as we can to make us more secure. We are told that if we get a good education, a good job, make more money, have a bigger car, a bigger house or form a good relationship, that all these things will give us that happiness and security we have been seeking.

When you come here, stop and question. Have a look at what you believe yourself to be. Just have a look at this seeming centre, this reference point, which I refer to as 'I' or 'me'. What is it? Where does it start? What is it composed of? Where is the centre that I believe to be me? Is it in this body anywhere? Is it in this mind? As soon as this questioning starts along these lines, things are bound to happen because the false cannot stand up to investigation. What we believed without question all our lives cannot stand up to it. It falls apart.

That 'I' thought has no substance of its own. It cannot stand on its own. It needs that pure intelligence or consciousness or awareness (whatever you like to call it) behind it before you can have a single thought. There is nobody here now, or at any other time, who can negate their beingness. No one can ever say 'I am not'.

That knowingness is what intelligence is, that activity of knowing; that knowingness is constantly there. It is prior to the thought 'I am'. There is no need to repeat, 'I am, I am, I am.' That beingness expresses itself through the thought 'I am'. Whether you are saying it or not, there is still that knowing that you are that beingness or livingness. That intelligence–energy is expressing itself effortlessly.

So, now, can you define for me 'living'?

Q: A succession of happenings?

That is an *expression* of living. What is living itself?

Q: Breathing!

That, too, is an *expression* of living.

Q: There is no word for it. This is it!

It is just like the wind. Can you show me the wind? All you can see about the wind is an expression of it. It is waving the flag. It is moving the grass. It is moving the branches of the trees or whatever it is moving. This livingness, you cannot define it! Why? Tell me why.

Q: *You can't see it, can't feel it.*

Why? Because you are separate from it when you try to name it. You are that! You are that livingness! So, livingness cannot be defined because you are that. All that can be defined is what appears in and on that livingness; in other words, some expression of it. So, that pure beingness or livingness is what you are. You are that livingness! Just like the eye cannot see itself, you can never grasp it with the mind.

Without that livingness, could anyone have a single thought? It contains the thinking. The thinking cannot contain it. This beingness, this sense of presence, it hasn't change from the time I can first remember. Looking back from here, I know it was the same sense of presence, of 'I am', when I was a little child. That sense of presence has not changed. It is untouched. It can never be touched. It is not touched by time. It has not grown older or younger. Why? Because it contains time. It is not touched by space. Why? Because it contains space. That is why it says in the *Gita*, 'The sword can't cut it, the fire can't burn it, the wind can't dry it and the water can't drown it'. Why? Because it contains all of this manifestation. There is no thing that can contain it or grasp it.

We see all the objects in this room here but we never take notice of the space. If it was not for the space, the volume, there would not be any room for the objects. Space is always there before the objects. To the mind, the objects are more attractive than the space. The space is no thing. It is the same with awareness. There could not be a single thought if you were not conscious or aware.

So if we know that the answer is not in the mind, what might happen?

Q: *We stop looking there.*

Yes, we can stop looking there. How many years have you been searching for the answer? How many years did we try to work it all out? The answers to life or livingness itself you've never found because it's not some thing that you can grasp and tuck away in some mental corner and go on living. We see that all that this self-centre is, is an image or an idea in the mind of a self that's got no substance. The answer is not in the mind. Can you seek in any other place than the mind?

Let's look again at the analogy of the iron in the fire. We put the iron in the fire. It will become red like the fire. It will become hot like the fire. If you grasp it, it will burn you like the fire. It takes on the attributes of the fire. Now, take it out of the fire; what will it do? Will it get red? Will it burn? It has no substance of its own. It has no power to do these things, to be red hot, to burn. It has no power of its own to do these things.

The same with this idea that I have about myself. If it wasn't for that pure intelligence in the background, I couldn't have a single thought. It can't stand on its own. Another way of putting it is: each one of you is seeing right now; you are hearing right now. Is that so? Tell me, does the ear say, 'I hear'? Or does the eye say, 'I see'? Does the backside sitting on the seat say, 'I feel'?

(*Silence*)

Well, does it?

Q: No.
(*General agreement*)

What says, 'I see', 'I hear', 'I feel'? Doesn't a thought come up translating what is happening as 'I see' or 'I hear'? Look at it from another angle. Does the idea in the mind 'I see' actually see? Does the idea in the mind 'I hear', hear? Or does the idea in the mind 'I feel ', does that feel?

Q: No.

The thought comes up after the seeing, after the hearing. It is all happening prior to the thinking, just as it is. So, you can see from that, it's like the piece of iron. It has taken on the attributes of that pure intelligence, which is registering everything as it is, and believes itself to have the power.

You can see from that, that added to this image of myself, it believes it has personal volition, personal power. In addition, it needs a God or something else to make it whole because things are not going the way it expects them to. If it had such power, why are things not going the way it wants it to, if it is running the show? The unlimited potential has limited itself into the shape or form of a poor miserable human being. And we live from that point until we see that we were never that.

All these pointers you will see when you start to question. You will see clearly that this idea or image that I have about myself is not what I really am at all. It is an idea based on past events and experiences. Not only does it have no reality as such but it's a dead image. It is based on yesterday, yesterday's events and happenings. There is no livingness in it whatsoever. As it appears and comes up, it comes up presently. Like the piece of iron in the fire, it is in the fire and heated by the fire. And so it is with the intelligence. The intelligence is heating up this idea, this image, and it believes itself to have the power. But it never did have!

In seeing that there is no centre here, then I'm free from that seeming bondage. The cage that I have built around myself, the cage of limitations, is that I believe myself to be a separate entity, a person, an individual. As soon as that idea of separation comes, there is immediate insecurity, immediate vulnerability, and the anxieties, fears, resentments, self-pity. And everything else must come from that image of separation because it is trying to make itself whole or complete. You are the timeless! Thought is time appearing on the timeless.

Looking from the other angle, right here, right now, everyone is breathing; everyone's heart is beating; blood is coursing around the body; hair is growing; fingernails are growing; cells are being replaced; food is being digested. Who is making any effort to do these? Is there any 'me' or idea in the mind saying, 'I have to take the next breath', 'I've got to beat my heart', 'I have to digest my food'? Or is it happening effortlessly? Is there an innate intrinsic intelligence, an energy within that manifestation of the body that is coursing the blood through your veins right now? Isn't it causing the diaphragm to draw down, bringing in the air, then pushing it up to expel the air? It is taking all the food and all these various things that are needed to these different cells.

You can feel that energy. You can feel it in your fingertips and in your toes, if you like to watch closely enough, to feel closely enough. You can feel it there, pulsating, throbbing. The livingness is pulsing and throbbing through this pattern of energy right now. Effortlessly. No one is making an effort to do it. It is even causing the thinking. That energy has to find outlets. It shines out of your eyes as the light by which you see the world. What effort are you making to see? What effort are you making for that light to be in your eyes? What effort to hear? That intelligence, that innate, intrinsic intelligence, which pulsates through this body, is registering everything, right here, right now, just as it is. There is a direct experience of this, right now. Just like a mirror reflects everything just as it is. Or like a camera takes a photograph, just as it is. You are hearing the cars going by. You are seeing the movements in this room, smelling any odours that are present. All is registered just as it is, and I mean just as it is. It is uncorrected, unmodified, unaltered, just purely and simply, as is.

The mind names things. There are gaps in the thoughts continually where it is starting and stopping within you. Seeing and knowing that, those gaps become longer. The seeing and the hearing can and do happen without the naming, just being registered as is.

It is not the nature of the mind to be simple. It will go on analysing—analysis paralysis—creating all sorts of stories just to perpetuate itself. The mind will come up and try to modify what is. It will try to correct it or alter it: 'I don't like this'. 'This is good'. 'This is bad'. Then there is a resistance to what is. The mind is translating what is being registered. You don't have to look very hard to see that any resistance is conflict.

So, the idea that 'I don't like this' is just an idea in the mind. What is it that I don't like? I don't like the chair or the table. How do I know that it's a chair or a table? I have named it from some previous experience. I'm no longer with what is; I'm with the name. The name I've given it is just another idea in the mind. So, the mind is in conflict with itself, a seeming energy blockage, a resistance to what is.

If it is just what is and there is no resistance to it, what is happening? There's no conflict there whatsoever and things just express as is. That doesn't mean you have to sit down and do something. Everything will be done, as is. But if the resistance comes up and 'I don't like this', then what happens? That thought gets hold of it and builds it up and builds it up and builds it up. So what starts off as a little resentment will build up until the energy will be such that it has to be acted on. It will come out as some activity, anger, violence or whatever.

This is where all 'my' problems arise, from that dualism of 'me' and the 'other'. That sense of separation, that insecurity, that 'me', fears the unknown. Because that 'me' is the separation, it constantly fears. It would rather stay in the old way, no matter how unpleasant it is. 'I'll stay here rather than step out into the unknown'. Take that step into the unknown, into the 'no thing' and see! An old saying is, 'Do the thing you fear, and the death of fear is certain.' Let the intuitive take over without the 'me' thinking it knows better.

So, I understand there is no 'me' from this point of view. It has been seen clearly. Then I also understand that there can be no 'you' as such either. So, if there is no 'me' and there is no 'you', who is superior? Or who is inferior? What would I want of yours?

In the East, cause and effect is called *karma*, and in the Christian religion, 'As ye sow, so shall ye reap'. Remove the cause, and what must happen to the effect? The effect must drop off also. There cannot be an effect without a cause. And that is all that simply has to happen. Without the mind, without the thinking, right now, snap off the thinking for just a moment. Or just keep the mind full by saying 'no mind, no thought', 'no mind, no thought'. Any thought other than that, just say 'no thought'.

While you were doing this, did you stop hearing, breathing, feeling or seeing? Realise from that, that everything was still being registered while the mind was occupied with the thought 'no thought'. That is another proof that you are not the mind.

The cause of all my problems is 'me', this self-centre, this image that everything is relative to. This dead image is not the livingness. It is based on yesterday. If the image is not there, then the livingness must be there in its fullness.

Don't you know that this intelligence has brought you through all the dramas and traumas and things that happen? It has brought you through that to right here and right now. Don't you know that it is going to continue? It will continue to look after this body–mind, this pattern of energy, for as long as the body–mind is going to be around. In this, without that effort, isn't there a great sense of freedom? Just the freedom to be, which I am anyway!

Chapter 5
Be What You Are

The cage of self-centredness, which I have built around myself, a cage of words, is a phantom. It does not exist! The cage door is open right now. As a matter of fact, the whole cage can be seen to be what it is and will fall away right now.

The cage of limitations. Words: good/bad, pleasant/painful, positive/negative, possible/impossible. All words! And the word is not the real. You can say 'water, water' for the rest of your life. Try to drink the word! The word is a symbol for something else. It is not the real. And yet when I say, 'I'm no good' or 'I have low self-esteem', what reality has it got? Or look at it the other way, 'I'm superior,' 'I'm better'. Is that what you are? What does that symbolize? Can it be there at all if there is no livingness?

Instead of trying to come up with an answer in the mind, wouldn't it be wise to just be with this livingness, to be with this beingness, to settle down with this presence? Watch how it is expressing: feeling it shining through your eyes, lighting up your face, feeling the breath; seeing it as it is; marvelling at the very fact of seeing, of all the variety and diversity that it can express; marvelling at all the different feelings that can come up in this way, instead of attaching to them and allowing them to build up until they get out of all proportion, until they have taken over exclusively the whole of that awareness and functioning, like a cloud covering the sun. We do this to the exclusion of everything else. We are seemingly lost in it.

When you stop stirring the water in the bucket, it becomes still. It doesn't matter what your story is: 'I should not have said that' or 'I should not have done such and such'. You're stirring the water! Full stop! Right here, right now!

Even while the thinking is going on, I can be seemingly deeply absorbed in it all. Realise that there is still the sensation of sitting. There is still the hearing of the cars going by and whatever else is being heard. There is still the tasting and the smelling.

Bring it back into its proper proportion. What room is there for any problems? Problems are seen as they arise. Activity takes place as necessary. Then what is the problem? I can ask any one of you right now: What is wrong with right now unless you think about it? There is an instant pause while you try to see what is wrong. Realise that before anything can be wrong, there has to be thought. So, come back to that constantly. Right here, right now, presently, there is nothing wrong. Just the same as, what past is there unless I think about it? What future is there unless I think about it?

I hear some say that they can't stand to stay in the 'right now': 'I can't stand it!' When do you ever leave right now? When is it ever not present? The mind creates an image of yesterday or imagines and anticipates a tomorrow. Time is a mental concept. Now we are back where we started. Right here, right now, there is no one that is not present and aware of that presence. Is that so?

Q: Yes! (General agreement)

Are there any questions?

Q: The mind is there. It operates. We don't have an alternative, so what is the answer?

The mind is a wonderful instrument when it is used rightly. All the art, the technology, and all the creativity—it all comes through that mind. Nisargadatta said, 'The mind is a good servant but a bad master'.

Q: So do we have to be taught how to utilize it?

No, just come back, realising presence. In this presence, everything is registering just as it is. Watching from that awareness, you will recognise when the mind begins to go into the past or the future. And that is the head trip. It's trying to alter what is. It is altering or modifying what is, and that is resistance. There will be recognition of your resistance to things, and that recognition must be from the point of no resistance. We just need to recognise that this is resistance or inattention. Inattention is recognised from the point of attention. There is no one to *be* attentive. Just notice that there is a little resistance or a little bit of inattention there.

In the moment of recognition, there is a subtle relaxation. From that moment, you are back in the moment with what is. Sooner or later, the recognition will come up again because now you are aware of it. Whereas before, it was just ignored totally and not even thought about. Now that it has been pointed out that there is no centre there, that there is no other time than presence, the intelligence sees this. And it sees when you are taken out of it.

Q: Do you meditate?

Attention to what is, is meditation. Sometimes I sit; sometimes I don't. There are long periods of silence here at times. And there will be periods of chatter. But both of them are experiences of the mind. I can only say that I have a silent mind or a chattering mind through experiencing it. What I am is prior to that. So it does not matter to me. I don't prefer one over the other. It does not make a difference; they are both what is.

Q: Where does action come in?

Action is spontaneous. It comes in in the presence.

Q: You don't try to regulate it, you don't try to direct it?

No, not at all. There is no one to direct it. It will be directed if that is what is necessary in the moment.

Q: It's a totally passive concept then?

Who is to be passive? If you say, 'I'm going to be passive', you are back in that self-centre. It is to be alert to what is, and that means you are totally with that activity of knowing and being, more so than you've ever been before. It is just like living with a snake in the room. You're going to watch its every move! You have no room for the head stuff. You'll be looking around taking in everything else that's going on. The head stuff takes its proper place. Each of the senses is allotted its proper place. But most of us are so used to being in the head that it has taken over the largest proportion and the other senses function only a little bit.

But if everything is in its proper sequence, what's going to be a problem about this? What is seen from a narrow viewpoint in the 'me', when seen from the totality, is something that can be handled, probably quite easily. And what will happen? Nobody knows!

Once the old habit patterns are seen, once you have seen that it is all habit patterns, it can never get the same intensity that it had before. The old habit patterns will continue for a while because they have been there for years and years as conditioned responses. But once they have lost their hold and the energy has gone out of them, they are not going to stay. There is no point in them.

Q: So, we just watch the thoughts?

You are prior to the thought. You are not the thought. Be aware of it. In that registering, in that pure intelligence, it is all being witnessed just as it is. As soon as there is some modification or correction, that is a thought. Now that is also just as it is. The next thought will be just as it is. The next movement, just as it is.

Q: How does this concept fit with planning? Is there no need for planning?

If that comes up right now, plan, set it up, do what you have to do now. But instead of carrying it around in your head, mulling over it, 'What will be the outcome?', etc., when the planned time becomes the present, act on it then. Carrying it around is weighing you down. Planning is part of living, just the same as the memory is there to be used. But when memory starts to use you, it becomes self-destructive! Memory is a very necessary thing. The mind is not the enemy!

But if you look at it in a different light and see, all the mind is, is a movement of energy, just the same as the whole manifestation. This manifestation is pure intelligence–energy vibrating into different patterns, different shapes, different forms. It is like the sunlight hitting the crystal. The light comes out as those colours, but what are those colours? Are they anything other than the sun's rays? So, this pure awareness is dancing around there as you, and here as Bob, and somebody else over there. Has it changed its true nature? After some time the crystal is moved or the sun's rays stop touching it. What happens? The rays are not shining through that particular form. Have they been lost?

Q: This is interesting!

The real interest is to come back to awareness–presence as quickly as possible. Its essence, its true nature, is that pure intelligence–energy. It can never be added to or taken away from. It is the changeless reality. So, we see that thinking patterns are energy. If the energy doesn't go into them, they drop off. Nothing gained, nothing lost, just what is.

Q: It's amazing how easy it is to make a decision without all that clutter going on.

It's easy enough for a decision to come up, isn't it? But then the clutter starts up again as to whether I have made the right decision.

(*Laughter*)

What is word? Word is sound. What is thought? Thought is subtle sound. Sound is vibration. Vibration is energy. The way it vibrates is in opposites: good/bad, pleasant/painful, past/future, positive/negative. All words!

Whatever comes through that pure intelligence, because it (the intelligence) is the reality, it cannot change. The definition of reality is: that which does not change. It's just like the mirror. A mirror will reflect everything in it, but no image in the mirror contaminates the mirror. So, that pure intelligence is not contaminated by any thought or feeling. When the mind realises that it has no power of itself, just like the piece of iron in the fire, then it aligns itself with that intelligence. It's the vehicle through which that expression comes, which must be put into words, ideas, plans or whatever. In other words, the mind is there for its proper function.

Q: This is where I have a problem, with planning and predicting a certain outcome.

With the idea of doing comes the 'me' that's going to do something about it. It starts up that self-centredness again. There was never any 'me' there in the first place. All that is done is done from that functioning.

Q: Wasn't there a 'me' to select the outcome?

Not really. Have a look and see what the 'me' is. See for yourself that there never was a 'me'. The 'me' is only an idea in your mind. If it has no substance, where is the bondage? Where is the self-centre? It is only the 'me' that is the cause of my problems. If I am not functioning from that false centre, then I must be with what is.

Q: Hard to accept in the first ten minutes.

(Everyone laughs and agrees)
We have years and years of habitually looking 'out there', outside of ourselves, ignoring our true nature. Our problem is ignorance. We ignore our true nature and go with what we are told: 'Johnny, you're a good little boy' or 'You're a bad little boy', 'You are this', that, and the other'. And added to that are all the events and experiences that happen. All this builds an image. This image is constantly changing, little bits being added to it, little bits taken away. And something is always affecting this image. We didn't ever stop to look!

Once you have seen it clearly, this true investigation, sitting with it and seeing the false as false, the image is then understood. It has no power of its own. It is known for certain. It is not a belief. As Christ said, 'Know the truth and the truth will set you free'.

Q: Was primitive man more in touch with it?

Not necessarily so. There would be those who were in touch with it as there always have been.

Whatever direction you go in from this presence, this 'now', must be in the mind, in the thought. If there is no thinking, what is wrong with right now? Is there any other thing than right now, if there is no thinking? It is always presence (omnipresence).

Q: For a period of time, my life has been going well, in comparison with what it was before. However, sometimes my mind will tell me I need something to happen to see how well I am. Why is that? Why, when things are going well, do I want to question things?

Here is a little story. There is this traveller in the desert. It's very, very hot, and he is thirsty. In the distance there is one lone tree. He doesn't know that it is a wishing tree. He goes and sits beneath it and he thinks, 'This is nice, I only wish I had a cool drink now'. Lo and behold, a cool drink appears in his hand. 'Oh! Terrific!', he says. 'Now if only I had a soft bed to lie on and drink this, with a bit of a breeze to fan me'.

Lo and behold, a soft bed appears, as well as a maiden with a fan, fanning him. 'Oh! This is terrific. Now all I need is a good meal to go with all this, and everything would be just right'. Lo and behold, a big meal appears. Then the mind says, 'Hey! What's all this? What's going on? Maybe it's the devil?' And the devil appears. The mind then says, 'Oh! He's going to eat me'. And he does!

So, when everything is going right, the mind, just on its own, wants to question. This is the usual pattern. The answer is not in the mind. Full stop! If you understand that, what direction can you take from that?

Q: No direction.

That's right. Full stop. Any direction you take must be in the mind.

Everything is being registered just as it is. All the impressions are coming in through the senses and being registered, just as is. The things that you have no vested interest in are of no concern whatsoever. If you got up and walked out of the room right now, you would step over those cushions. You wouldn't kick them out of the way. You would step over them quite naturally. That means it is all being registered without your thinking about it.

Realising that this intelligence is functioning, that's the 'razor's edge'. That is functioning. The mind comes in and wants to discriminate, to modify it, alter it or correct it in some form or another. You can rely on that pure intelligence that is effortlessly functioning in that body right now.

There is no centre here. You must see the falseness of it. You must see that it has no power of its own. And this can happen only by looking, by investigating. Stay with the awareness. Let what that essence is reveal itself to you without that 'me' being in the way. There is livingness. There is beingness. There is awareness of that being present, just as it is. This is what we call effortless living. You are being lived effortlessly. Nobody tells the stomach to digest the food!

Q: Even the awareness, it just is? That attentiveness, it just is?

Yes!

Q: Bob, is this like a surrendering?

Well, have a look, George, and see. What is it that needs to surrender?

Q: I suppose we surrender the ego.

Have a look at that. Is there such a thing?

Q: No, there is not.

Well, how can you surrender something that is not there? When you see that it is false and that it never existed, you don't have to surrender. Full stop. See that clearly!

Q: I try to bring myself in, in my mind, and it's a struggle.

Let it go!

Q: Is it because it is unseen that we try to label it?

Yes, the mind has to try to grasp something. It tries to give it a concept, an image. This it cannot grasp. So it will create all sorts of things. It will even create a next life. 'At some future time, if I have been a good boy that has created a God and a heaven, I'll go up there' (*pointing upwards*). Or, if it's in the East, 'I'll come back, I'll reincarnate'. It's always becoming, instead of being. Becoming is some projected future time when things will be. There is no future time to become in. The actuality is right now. This is the livingness. You can never live this moment again—this moment, right now.

Q: Where does the energy go when we die?

Where does a wave go when it drops back into the ocean?

Q: I don't know.

Will that same wave come out again? No.

Q: Where does the energy come from?

(*Tapping his lower chest*) This is called the solar plexus. Why? The ancients called it the sun plexus. That is where this energy radiates out, just like the sun radiates and gives life to the Earth. This solar plexus is not contained in the body. It animates the body. It is the life. It lives the body. The sun is the very life. It's the energy, the light, the heat. Without it, there would not be anything. Energy comes into the body through the breath and goes out through the breath. This energy goes all through the body to the ends of your toes and fingers. It also radiates out to all those around you.

You are not the body. You are not the mind. So, what is the body? Now, when that sperm and ovum meet, that consciousness, that livingness, that cell doubles and redoubles. That little embryo starts to expand, and the energy in it starts to spread and grow in the mother. The heart starts beating before the brain is even formed. How can there be any 'I' for it there? It attunes itself to that warmth, the heartbeat and the breathing of the mother. It is growing itself effortlessly. Again, this is proof that this 'I' thought, this idea or image, of itself, has no power whatsoever. It is powerless. That is not what I am.

Realise that this is what is happening. You are being lived. You are that livingness itself.

Q: Nothing can happen to a 'non-me'. Everything just happens because I'm not a 'me'.

Live from that point of view and see. You will then start to see some of the scriptural statements start to come true. 'A thousand shall fall at thy side and ten thousand at thy right hand; but none shall come nigh thy dwelling place'. I see this constantly. The world is still going on, but there is very little that comes here. What can come here is handled— simply, easily and effortlessly. Whereas before ... I can re- member a few years back, when I was involved in the whole bloody lot, and it was destroying me!

But if you are that pure intelligence, what can be added to you?

Q: Nothing!

What can be taken away?

Q: Nothing!

When you are hungry, doesn't something let you know? When you need to go to the toilet, doesn't something let you know? This so-called individual innately and intrinsi- cally knows it already. But in its own mind it can't grasp it. So, it creates an image out there, which has to 'hear it' (the knowledge).

All problems are problems of relationship: 'me' and 'other'. If there is no relationship, what might happen? A so- called energy level or wavelength will be attracted to you as is necessary in the pattern of energies—just like the bees are attracted to the flower to pollinate—to express and recreate and rebuild this life.

There is only life—only life! There is no death. Life lives on life. When this so-called body breaks down, there is still life going on because enzymes and microbes begin to change the pattern. If the body is burnt, it is reduced to ashes. And these go back into the elements they came from. What is lost? The expression, the appearance or pattern is changed. Is that intelligence this energy is—is that lost? Knowing that, is there anything to fear?

Q: What is this fear that I feel?

If you look at it fresh and new without naming it, is it then fear? As soon as you say 'It's fear', you're naming it from the past. The natural thing to do, as we have always done, is to try to avoid fear. The mind shuts off and tries to move away from it. It tries to create something else, instead of being with what is. So, you are trying to alter or modify 'what is' in some way. If you look at it, stay with it, go through it, see exactly what it is, then see how it is.

Q: *There is nothing to need.*

Needs are taken care of as necessary for the functioning.

Q: *You have a lot better use of the energy.*

Yes. If that energy is not going on in the so-called personal chatter, then it is there to be utilized in the moment, expressing it. That thought 'I am' is in the mind. That thought is what was born and that is what dies. The mind wants to perpetuate itself. The mind is a wonderful instrument. It is not the enemy. It doesn't have to be forcefully shut out or closed.

Q: *What is desire?*

Desire is the fixation of the mind on an idea. Get out of its groove by denying it attention. The seeming doer goes on until you see that there is no doer.

Q: *It is the nature of the mind to perpetuate its own identity.*

Yes.

Q: *So, when the body passes and the mind passes, there is death.*

Yes. That thought 'I am' is what was born, and that is what dies. In St. Francis' prayer it says, 'For it is only by dying that I can have eternal life'. He was not talking about the physical death. It is about dying to that sense of self, that 'me'.

St. Paul said, 'I die daily'. It is dying to that idea of mind. It just has to be understood. Nisargadatta says, 'Understanding is all'.

As children we have put upon us the idea of an ideal person. It's generally Christ or Buddha or one of the others. Those who put this idea onto us can't live up to it themselves. We get the idea that 'I should be like this' or 'I shouldn't be like that', and that is added to this image that we have about ourselves. This image of an ideal person leads to the feeling 'I'm not good enough' or 'My self-esteem is low'. This is one of the greatest causes of our problems. It has been imposed on us by others who never lived up to it either.

Each one of us is intelligence expressing itself. Each one is a unique expression. No two expressions are the same. In all of the diversity within this cosmos or the manifestation of the universe, each point of expression is unique. So, a thought such as 'how I should be' becomes a limiting factor, when you are that unique expression already.

Stop pretending to be what you are not. Be what you are! Just be! So relax. Be open. Be open in the heart. It resonates. It is recognised. It is known. It is pure, simple, understanding.

Q: Is there more than one 'I'?

There is not even one 'I'.

Q: But I mean 'to the mind', because there seems to be multiples.

Where is that appearing? In the mind! But then the mind will say, 'I don't like this' (whatever this is at any particular time). So, you see, this idea 'I don't like this' becomes a reference point. This reference point jumps in and creates another reference point, trying to escape the first reference point. That's where the feeling comes up that there is more than one 'I'. The mind will swap reference points continually. This is the nature of the mind. Investigate and find that there is no particular point where you can say 'This is where it all started'.

By continuously seeing the mind, it loses its power, its intensity. Then it's there for what it is meant to be there for. Break that habit pattern of 'Oh, but' and 'If' and 'I know from past experience'. That is what comes in through the mind, and we lose our spontaneity and the intuitiveness. The sixth sense is sometimes called the spiritual sense. It will come up spontaneously, but the mind will say, 'Oh no, I've got something better'.

Q: Where does the duality start?

The habit pattern or that belief that I am the doer!

Q: I don't have the courage to accept that I am not controlling my life.

See the limitation you place on it. What is intelligence and energy? Isn't it courage itself? Isn't it love itself, compassion itself? You have all the courage you need. But we put the limitation on it by 'I don't have the courage', etc. Once it is seen clearly that there is no centre here, even if you get caught in the habit patterns again, you only *seemingly* have lost it. In the knowing and the deep underlying reality of knowing, this is never lost. There is no beginning to it. There is no ending to it. Is there any separation? Are you separate from the air you breathe? Are you separate from the earth you stand on? What is this separation? Is it just another concept?

Chapter 6

The Mind Cannot Change the Mind

Q: What is the nature of your teaching?

This teaching embraces Advaita Vedanta. It embraces Kashmir Shaivism. It embraces Dzogchen, the highest form of Buddhism. And it embraces the highest form of Christianity, too.

It is just that non-duality, the one-without-a-second, or as it is said in Christian religion, omniscience, omnipotence and omnipresence. There is nothing other than That. If there is nothing other than That, who is the guru and who is the disciple? It is all That. We know this in our language. For instance, that is a chair, that is a cup, that is John. Take the words 'chair', 'cup' and 'John' away, and what is it? It is all That. There is nothing other than That. I am That. Thou art That. That is That.

Q: What about the word 'God'? Are you comfortable with that word?

That all depends on the concept. You see, the word 'God' has a lot of different concepts for a lot of different people. With some it is Christ and with others it is Buddha, and with others it is something else. If God is omniscience, omnipotence and omnipresence, that is all-knowing, all-being and all-presence. I don't like to use that term, 'God' because the recipients aligns it with their image or a definition. I prefer to call it intelligence–energy.

We are told that we are a person, that we are a separate individual or a separate entity. And naturally, it is believed from then on. When you are a little child, before the reasoning starts, it is not 'I do this or that'. It is 'Johnny does this' or 'Johnny wants that' (whatever the name may be). Johnny does not see himself as a separate entity. Then, after a while, it becomes 'I'. The thinking process seemingly forms the individual. With the registration of everything, everything is just as it is. All the thinking, the seeing, the hearing, the smelling, tasting and touch sensations are registered in the immediacy of this moment. But then, as soon as the thought 'I' see' or 'I' hear' or 'I' think' comes up, who does it refer to?

You see that 'I' in its purity cannot refer to anything. So, added to it with that thinking process is the image you have from your conditioning and from memory. That image is what you believe yourself to be. As soon as you say 'I am John' or 'I am Bob' or whatever your name is, there immediately comes in the associated conditioning 'I am good' or 'I am bad' or 'I am special' or whatever the conditioning is; for example, 'I am happy' or 'I am unhappy' or 'I am a doctor', or 'I am only a labourer and I'll never get anywhere in life'—whatever your belief or whatever the conditioning is that has happened in your life.

That 'I' thought is the separating factor. The way the mind functions is only in the pairs of opposites. As soon as that 'I' comes up, there has to arise a 'you' or the 'other', something other than 'I'. The very idea of that 'I' thought immediately implies separation. It implies isolation. That is vulnerability. That is fear.

Q: How do you see through this appearance of six billion separate individuals?

By investigation, by trying to find out in the first place who is this 'I', who is this 'me'? Is it what I think I am? Is it what I believe myself to be? What is that 'I' thought? Stay with it. To the mind it is 'no thing'. It is not the nature of the mind to stay with 'no thing'. The mind has to have some image or some appearance or thing to keep it going. In staying with that 'no thing' for an instant, the idea of fear arises, a fear that 'I am going to lose my reason', 'I am going to lose my identity'. It is seemingly hard to stay with 'no thing' because the nature of the mind is to think. It is a movement of energy. It is moving back and forth constantly. To stay with 'no thing' means no energy is going into the thinking. So, thinking cannot happen without energy.

Q: A lot of teachers say that there is no doership and that all is destiny. But you say that there is something you can do, and that is to stay with the question 'Who am I?'

Yes, but who is the doer? When you talk about destiny, destiny for whom? Who is it that needs to stick to the question of 'Who am I?'

The only instrument that pure intelligence has got is this thinking mind. Intelligence functioning through the mind is nothing but that pure intelligence vibrating into a pattern, which we call thought. We attribute these thoughts to a 'me' or a separate entity. They are nothing other than this pure intelligence–energy. Investigate and see that it is so.

Q: What would you tell somebody who believed that they were still an individual, believed that they were a personality with a name attached to it? What would you tell them to do?

Well, if someone were to come to me and say 'I am seeking truth or reality', I would say, 'What you are seeking you already are!' So it is foolish to carry on the search. The only place the search started from is in the mind. It can't start anywhere else, and it can't continue anywhere else than in the mind. When I realise, or when it is pointed out, that it is foolish to carry on the search in the mind, what must happen? If I say to you, 'Full stop; the search is over', what would you do? Wouldn't there be a pause? In that pause wouldn't there be a realisation that 'I have not disappeared', 'I have not fallen apart', 'I have not disintegrated', 'I am still here without that thinking mind'? Then there must be a glimpse of understanding that everything that we seemingly believe relies on that mind.

Without that mind, the functioning is still happening.

You're still breathing, hearing, seeing, thinking, tasting, touching and smelling. Livingness is still happening without the mind seemingly running the show, which it has done for years. Once that glimpse is there, that there is functioning happening, it is seen as a place of stillness. This is the aim of meditators, to quiet the mind to that place of stillness. I say that is the wrong way because to quiet the mind, you have to use the mind to quiet the mind, and all that is, is conflict in the mind. It is one thought fighting against another thought.

In just the seeing of the fact that there is no answer in the mind, you are free of it. It is just like you come up here to look for your watch when you know that you left it in the kitchen. It is foolish to look up here. In the twenty or thirty years that you have been seeking, looking for the answer in the mind, you have never found it. However, you are not an idiot because you have solved a lot of other problems through the mind. But you have not found the answer to life in the mind. Surely there must come a time when you realise that it is futile to look in the mind, especially when the traditions tell you that the answer is not there.

Q: In terms of the futility of looking in the mind, what you always say is that the false cannot stand up to investigation. So how do we start to investigate?

Come back to the only reality that you are absolutely certain of—the fact of your own being. Everything else is a mental concept. But you cannot negate your beingness. Stay with that beingness or the thought 'I am', which is the nearest thing you can get to beingness with the mind. That is the primary thought. Stay with that, come back to that.

Q: How do you define staying with the thought 'I am'?

Whenever it moves away to 'I am this' or 'I am that', bring it back to just 'I am'. Also have an affectionate awareness of just being 'I am'. Be warm towards that 'I am-ness'. Love that 'I am-ness'. That is the first point where the mind comes into it. You will realise after a while that you do not have to say 'I am' to know that you are. You have known this all the time. You don't go around saying 'I am', I am' repeatedly. You are still functioning, livingness is still going on, other thoughts are coming in, other activities are taking place, but it all comes back to that sense of presence that expresses through the mind as the thought 'I am'. That is the only reality that you cannot negate.

Stay with that long enough, be affectionate towards it, then there is a seeming response to that warmness. That warmness may only be a mental warmness, but there will be a seeming response to that warmness, and that warmness will well up through your beingness, through your body and through the mind. It will suffuse that beingness and bring about the change that is necessary.

Q: It is as if it is acknowledged.

Exactly. That is a beautiful way to put it. There is a passage in the Bible that says: 'Acknowledge Him in all thy ways and He will direct thy path'. Most of us interpret that as somebody out there, but it means to acknowledge that essence, that intelligence that you are. In acknowledging that, the direction comes through that.

Q: I would like to stay with the subtlety of this 'I am'. Can you say more about this?

Have a closer look at 'I am'. It is not 'I was', nor is it 'I will be'. It is expressing that presence. It is pure presence. 'I am'. Presence! Not the past, not the future. The actuality is always now. You do not have to use the term 'I am'. You see, that primary thought 'I am' is too subtle for the mind to grasp, so it adds to it 'I am this', 'I am that', 'I am the fear', 'I am the anger', 'I am the anxiety, depression' or whatever. Just see that thought as the expression of that presence.

Then what must you be? You must be that presence. That is all that there is. It is omnipresence.

These words are presence. That is how they are appearing. They are appearing presently. As you hear these words, they are appearing presently. This chair I am sitting in is presence. You are presence. Everything is presence. It is all That. We take the appearance as real rather than seeing its essence, which is presence.

Q: There is no process of awakening to this understanding. Is that right?

Yes, that is right. If it is omnipotence, omniscience and omnipresence, when have we, and who has ever, been separate from it? When and how could there be any separation from it? If that idea of separation is seen for what it is, an erroneous belief, a phantom, what process could there be?

We have hypnotized ourselves into believing that we are this separate 'I', this separate entity, this individual. That is not going to die down overnight or immediately. The seeing of it is immediate, but the old habit patterns will come up again and again because patterns are repetition—repeating thought patterns of who and what we think we are. The continuity of thought becomes feeling and emotion. It all has gone on so frequently and for so long, and that is why it will not just disappear overnight.

Q: These sentient beings called humans have been around for tens of thousands of years. Are you saying that they are all wrong?

I know that I was wrong in believing I was a sentient human being. And from that I have freedom from all those erroneous beliefs. I am not the only one. I have read various books, and from that can see that all through the ages there have always been so-called people with this understanding. They have carried this message through those tens of thousands of years, and they go right back to the so-called mythical primal guru from the beginning of time.

Q: You often quote Christ where he said 'I am the light of the world'.

'I am the way; I am the truth; I am the light', not meaning himself. He means come back to that 'I am'.

Q: That is your interpretation.

Yes, that is my interpretation.

Q: Who is that 'me' or 'my'?

That is just the terms we use in conversation. I am not afraid to use the words. I use the words just the same as they have always been used. Just the same as I will use the words 'What a beautiful blue sky', knowing full well that the sky is not blue. It only appears to be blue. I know full well that there is no centre here, no 'me'. It is quite simple. The false cannot stand up to investigation. The mind will make up all sorts of tricks. It will invent a subconscious, a super-conscious, and all sorts of different degrees and levels of the mind. And it will seek the answer there. As I say, there have been people all through those thousands of years who have said, 'Come back to where it all begins, that beingness'.

Q: So, in that recognition of inattention, when you recognise that you are not just attentive to awareness, there is no guilt. There is freedom in that recognition. You are.

Exactly!

Q: Although I no longer believe in a process, it still seems that the more time I spend being aware of awareness, something continually feels like it is opening. It is almost like the perception gets wider, subtler.

Exactly. And with that you would find that the thought processes are lessening.

Q: There is an absence of thinking a lot of the time.

In that absence of thinking, what must you be with? Pure awareness or pure consciousness. Then, as the range expands, everything is taken in. Less and less is excluded, the perception is wider and wider, and the greater the perception is of what is.

What is, is pure intelligence–energy registering everything just as it is. There is no thinking process in that. The thinking process will alter, modify or correct what is registering. To do that, it must refer to a past event, image or experience, which is the 'me'. So, then, everything is relative to that 'me', the self-centre.

Now, if it is not relative to that, if it is just what is, then what can you say about it, and what is wrong with it? Isn't it functioning and expressing beautifully as is? Everything appears on that pure presence–awareness. That is just a pure registering, and there is no experience in that whatsoever.

Q: So a preference for silence through meditation is missing the point?

How can I prefer the silence to the chatter? What difference do either make when they are appearance only? Nothing has touched that awareness that I am. Nothing can contaminate it, and nothing can come near it. It is bodiless, mindless, birthless, deathless.

Q: How would you describe awareness without using the words 'I am' or 'a sense of presence'?

Pure awareness, pure registering of what is. You're hearing right now; seeing right now. Everything is registering just as it is. That doesn't mean to say everything is a homogenous blob. Everything is distinguished and registered, but it is not named. It is not given a name. It is just as is.

Q: What is it that makes us begin to search for truth?

The seeming search comes from the idea of separation. As soon as that 'I' thought comes up, that 'I' implies separation. Separation is insecurity, vulnerability. There is immediate insecurity with that 'I' thought. That separation is only a seeming separation. It is only how it appears. Anything in this manifestation can be broken down into pure energy. If this globe called the Earth were to be blown into little pieces, would any of the energy be lost? The Earth is gone, but would anything be lost? It would all be out there in space. Nothing would be lost.

Q: So the individual is just a bundle of memories that is seemingly separate. However, there appears to be immense diversity in the guise of individuals.

Exactly. And even those seeming individuals are in the pairs of opposites—male and female. And that attraction brings them together to carry on this diverse appearance. But what has happened really? Nothing! So if you know that nothing has happened, are you going to leave the play? It is just like if you're in a stage production playing the villain. When you know that you are playing a role, as soon as the play is over, you take off the make-up, your mask or disguise, and go home and have a good sleep. So, when you see that all that is going on is a play of consciousness, then you still take part in the role as a seeming individual, knowing the truth about it, that there is no such thing as an individual. The very idea of an individual implies something as being separate from something else.

This is confronting to many, based on belief. Any belief or non-belief becomes a reference point. And everything is judged from that point of view. Then that becomes another self-centre or reference point, just the same as the 'I' or the 'me'. So, here in this body–mind, there are no set beliefs and there are no set opinions. I can have opinions, but they are not set in concrete. Just the same as I can say 'I' or 'me' and that is not set either.

Q: What about the room full of seekers and the guru? Even in this understanding there still is something going on, in that there is the guru and a bunch of seekers. Isn't there some way of transcending that?

The way, for those people that come along, is to immediately see themselves as equal. I can speak about this for the rest of my life, and there will still be millions that won't see the truth in it. They must test it for themselves.

Q: So many seem to miss this suggestion to look for themselves, to ask the questions of themselves and let the intelligence–energy come up within themselves. It took five months for me to hear your suggestion and actually try it.

Yes, but the difference with you is that you kept coming back! It was the same in my case. It went on for years and years until I arrived in the presence of Nisargadatta. By this time, I had to look. By this time, with all the seeking in the mind and all the kundalini and spiritual experiences ... As I say, you can have many, many spiritual experiences, but there is only one spiritual awakening. Those experiences are like the carrot before the donkey. They were leading me on more and more. That can be a trap, too, because you can just want the experiences. But, seemingly, somewhere along the line, the mind seemed to get fed up with it all, and it packed up. Then the truth was there ready and waiting, as it always had been, to rush into that little gap and take over.

Q: This misconception of enlightenment where there is as if some place to attain, some place to be ...

What is there or who is there to be enlightened? It is only this 'me' that believes itself to be unenlightened or not whole or not complete. If you look at that, you will see that this 'me' is only an image. It is an idea. Of itself it cannot see. It cannot be aware. It has no power whatsoever. So, how can that thought, which has no power, ever become whole or complete? By its very nature, the nature of thinking is to divide. All that the thinking process is, is division into the pairs of opposites. If its very nature is to divide, then how can it become whole? You must be able to see that the only time it can become whole is when there is no thought. Then the wholeness is there, which was always there.

Q: When we hear this message, quite often we set out on a quest to have no thought.

Yes, which is wrong again, because it is just a matter of seeing thought and understanding the way it functions. Then it has lost its hold. You see that the 'me' can't change anything. The 'me' is the mind, and the mind cannot change the mind.

Q: There are many seekers who are offended by this concept of non-doership. You are not driven to change anything.

You are not driven to change anything. But if that activity comes up where I am participating in change, then that is what is happening. That is what has been happening for the last twenty years, sitting here seemingly participating in changing seeming individuals and as a seeming person sitting here doing it. Nothing is really happening.

Q: The world is on a self-improvement quest now. What about that?

It is all based again on that seeming self-centre, 'me', and the 'other'. You see, as soon as there is a 'me', which is a reference point, then there must be the 'other'. If there is anger, then there is only a 'me' that can be angry. If there is fear, then it can only be a 'me' that can be fearful. If there is a seeming depression, then it can only be a 'me' that can be depressed. That 'me' is based on the past.

   If I see clearly that the 'me' is only an idea, an idea or image—it is not the centre, it is not solid, there is nothing solid there, there is no centre there—then, when these things come up, they are seen in a new light. So, it is a fresh and new experience that is happening right now: being identified as 'me', and then as they arise, they are named as 'fear' or 'depression' from the past. They are immediately named. But if it is seen and not named, then what happens to it?

Q: It begins to fade.

Even if doubt arises about this, if that is seen clearly as another idea, another thought, then no problem. Who is doubting? The mind comes up stronger, fighting to keep its seeming hold on you. But if it is looked at in every shape and every form and from every direction, if the falseness of it is constantly seen, then there is no way that it can ever take hold.

The mind is functioning here now with these words coming out. It has to. Thought is expressed as words. Immediately as it comes out, it is finished. There is no carrying on, like 'Did I say the right thing?', 'Does that sound correct?' You see, there is no reference point that it is constantly referred to.

Q: Who are we to each other?

Consciousness is speaking to consciousness. How else could it be? Can you conceive of or perceive of anything outside of consciousness? No. So, all this manifestation must be the content of consciousness. Now, can the content of consciousness be different from consciousness? It is consciousness speaking to consciousness, awareness speaking to awareness—intelligence–energy.

Q: A lot of people give themselves a hard time thinking that they could or should have done it better and that life has not given them the tools to get through the situations they are in. How does this help them?

It does not help them at all. It is the same in my own case. Years ago I thought the same. Now I see how beautifully it all fitted in. The pain, the fear, the anger and violence, the resentment, the self-pity, the greed, the envy—all these things had their place or I wouldn't be sitting here today. These things that I carried around with me for years, I am glad they happened, but there is no one to be glad, either. You see what I am trying to get at? They happened the way they happened.

Q: What about thought? How would you explain thought?

What is a thought? Thought is only a movement of energy. It is only energy expressing as a thought, then another thought. The same applies to a belief. All thoughts come and go. They appear and then disappear. You are prior to thought. All of the appearance is transient. In the immediacy of this moment, everything is registered as it is. It is seen. There is only one reality: Thou art That. The world is real, but not as it appears.

Q: A lot of us seem to suffer from what we think life should be like.

Yes. Life is! The same as what is. It is not what I think it should be. Life is. If you look at it closely, life lives on life. There is no death; life cannot know death.

Q: You would agree that when the body dies, the body ceases to function. But that is not death, because the energy cannot go anywhere.

The pattern of energy breaks down, but life is there in the breaking-down process. Another pattern will appear.

Q: When I look into myself I see no thing.

By what light do you see the 'no thing'? What is light? Light is knowing. Light is energy. You are the light! It shines of itself, just like the sun. The sun cannot know darkness. The further out it shines, the further darkness recedes. It cannot know light either, because there is nothing to compare it with. It shines of itself.

And so that knowingness and beingness shines of itself, also. That energy comes up and shines and focuses through the eyes. All the energy in the actuality of the moment is with what is. If the energy is going into resistance, then there is conflict; there is friction. The energy is seemingly fighting with itself. Trying to fix something is resistance, and the friction from that dissipates the energy. That also is just what is.

Chapter 7
No Thing

Q: What can the reader find in this book?

Following the book, if they have a look at themselves, they will see that they are not what they believed themselves to be in the first place. That will bring them to the understanding or the knowing that they are not that separate entity that is the cause of all their problems. If the cause is seen to be false, then what effect can there be? So, the so-called psychological suffering that humans go through will drop away. It is not necessary.

Q: In this understanding, when it opens up, what happens to all the memories and expectations of the future?

Memories are still there and can be brought into the moment. Memory is a good thing when it is utilized. All the beliefs of the separate entity fall away, and you realise that things have happened the way they have happened not because of any personal doership. With regard to the expectations of the future, there is no concern about that. Why be concerned with something that hasn't happened, when you can be with the actuality? The livingness is right now. All the vitality is in that. Why waste time with something that hasn't happened when you can be with what is—totally?

When the conditioning comes upon us, we seemingly lose sight of our true nature. But when it is pointed to, it is seen again, and it is no longer ignored. You know that you really have never left it. The true nature is 'no thing', but it is the unlimited potential in which all things appear and disappear.

Q: You have found various writings from different traditions that resonate with this understanding. Can you say anything about those writings?

Well, the first one that sort of opened me up was the *Advadhuta Gita,* when I was in the ashram. I knew there was something in that but couldn't quite grasp it. I used to love going back to it and reading it. Then after Nisargadatta, it was very clear. From then on, the things that I read only confirmed it. They might be saying the same thing in different words and in a different way. All they did was confirm what I already knew.

Q: What were some of the other writings you found?

A lot of the Dzogchen scriptures and other ancient scriptures, including Sengtsan from the Zen tradition. Some of these scriptures are put so beautifully. They point to this constantly. They are just flowing from the source. You can see it.

Another scripture says, 'Be thought-free'. A lot of people are mistaken about this as well. They think they have to throw out this thought and the next one, not thinking let the thought be free, let it do what it likes. Just like the clouds are not attached to the sky, they move on.

Q: When I see that the mind is never satisfied and relentlessly tries to capture the knowledge of the present, and wants to store it away and go on to search for something else imagining that it now has it, I see that it is completely useless. All I need to be is this immediacy.

Well, you can't be anything else! But we don't realise it. You see, it is omnipresence. So it can't be anything other than That.

Look at those memories from childhood. How do you know those moments? Did you have the same body as you do now? Did you have the same image that you have about yourself now? No. You know it because it is that innate intelligence, and that hasn't changed. That is the definition of reality: that which never changes. The body has changed, the image of yourself has changed, and the reference point or self-centre has changed, but That hasn't.

The whole manifestation is constantly changing. Everything is That, appearing as different. That is difficult for the mind to get a hold on. The mind is time and space. But That has no time. It is beginningless and endless. It has no space. It has no dimension. So the mind can never grasp it. The so-called 'a moment ago' has not left this omnipresence, though it appears to have. We give that appearance some distance. I can say 'a moment ago' or a 'year ago', but what are you doing? You only have to have a concept of 'a moment ago' and then have a concept of 'a year ago'. Then try to have a concept of 'a thousand years ago'. What is the difference?

You are the movement. Without a reference point, where can you say it starts from? Everything you see is objective. Everything you think is an object. You're aware of thinking, so it is an object. But we don't include this body–mind as an object. We think we are that which is seeing objects. We think we are the subject. But when I see you, I am seeing an object. So you are just an object, also.

When you realise that of yourself—'I am only an object also'—then there is just seeing. This is because we can't separate the seeing. When you look out anywhere you see 'no thing'. Yet it is seen. What can you call it, that which is seen, if you don't label it? You can't call it anything, so it is 'no thing'. So what you are actually seeing is 'no thing'.

Look at it this way: try to show me space. You can't, but you are seeing it! We are not registering it as a thing. There is no time that you are not seeing it.

Know that you are never distracted. You are never away from That. You can't seemingly forget it because, when you are seemingly forgetting it, that is it also.

Q: What is the bottom line?

The bottom line is: right here, right now, you are present and you are aware of being present. Realise that you are that one-without-a-second, pure presence–awareness, and *be what you are.*

Chapter 8
Open to This

Q: Awareness gets obscured. Why?

Where does the focus go when you think it (awareness) is obscured?

Q: Into thought.

But where is the thought appearing?

Q: On that awareness.

So, it really isn't obscured, is it? There is still hearing going on; there is still seeing. There is still cognising going on. Everything is still being cognised. In the immediacy of that, we are not taking notice of what is being cognised.

See your innate awareness right now. Just take a look over there (*points across the room*). You're seeing what you call the mirror over there. In the immediacy of right now it is being cognised, isn't it, before it is re-cognised. To re-cognise it, you have to use a label, 'That is the mirror'.

Q: Oh! I see.

At that moment you go into the 'past', memory. You will notice that cognising is happening in all-time, right now. You are hearing right now. You are hearing this voice, those cars passing by. When you say to yourself, 'Oh, that is a car passing by', if you look at that closely, you will see that *that* is being cognised also in the immediacy.

The thoughts that come up, 'I have lost it' or 'I am away from it', those thoughts are also being cognized. In other words, that cognising factor hasn't changed at all. Then it is re-cognised from memory. You see, we know what everything is. To re-cognise it we put the label on it. Do you understand that?

Q: Yes.

Well, that is the awareness that you are. Look at that awareness. For example, look at the mirror over there. Now, that mirror is appearing in awareness. Did awareness go over there for it to appear in? (*Pause*) Well, did it?

Q: No.

Right, so awareness is like the screen on which everything is appearing. Look up there (*points up*)—there is awareness. Look down there (*points down*)—there is awareness. Wherever you look, whatever you are seeing, it is always the content of that awareness. That is why they use the concept 'space-like awareness'. Everything is the content of space, isn't it? There is nothing that you can postulate or think of that is outside of space. So in essence it is all really space.

The same with this awareness. Even with space, there is an awareness of space. Think of the vastness of space. Awareness seems localised in this pattern of energy called a body—until it is investigated. When you investigate it, can you find a centre or a reference point that has any substance or any independent nature? When you look at your reference points, you see that they are all mental stuff. They are all mental images. The reference points are appearances on awareness, just the same as everything else is appearances. Appearances are taken to be real or concrete, something solid or substantial.

Q: But this (indicating her body) *is more than just thought. It is a sensory thing as well. This is just as real to me as awareness.*

Yes, but break it down. What is it made up of?

Q: Molecules.

Prior to that it is made up from the elements, isn't it? The air around you is an element. The space around you is another element. Fire, water are elements. That is what the body is made up of. But they can be broken down, also. Take water, for instance. You have water vapour, steam or cloud. At that level, cloud disperses into nothing, doesn't it? The next level has more density as it turns into water. The next level it changes to ice. Now, as ice you can carve it into a form of a human being or whatever. Now it has the shape and form of something that is seemingly solid and substantial. Put some heat on it, and it is back to water again. Put a bit more heat on it, and it has gone into mist again. You can call it ice and believe it is ice, but you know that if heat is applied to it, it disappears. It really is insubstantial.

Q: How is the body like ice? There is a border around the body.

Isn't there a border around ice? The ice cube has the shape and form of an ice cube.

Q: When the body dies it goes back into the elements?

Yes, back into the elements. If you know and understand it, it is there as an appearance. The functioning seems to happens from there (the body). But you know that it has no substance or independent nature, of itself. How would the ice be without the water in it?

Q: It couldn't be there.

Q (from another listener): When I say the person in this body thinks, it is a reference point.

That is where the trap is, because there is no person to think or be contained in it.

Q: I have only got my perception. I can only see from where I am.

Yes.

Q: Others may see something quite different.

Each pattern of energy is a unique pattern. It will manifest in all possibilities, in patterns we have not even thought of. But it still hasn't changed its true nature. That is why they say that there is no difference between a Buddha and an ordinary being. Both are made up of the elements. It is the same consciousness or awareness that is functioning through both of them and everything else.

Q: Something you said last week about being aware of thinking about the future has made a huge difference for me. It is so freeing. I see it in the right now, this thinking of a future.

So that is a little realisation, and it is yours now. You know it.

Q: Yes, I was trying to stop my mind from thinking of the past or future and that wasn't the way. Then I just became aware while the thinking of the future was happening. And it just dissipates. So just being aware of it is freeing.

Yes. When you see that you are trying to stop it with the mind, you see that that is just another thought, a conflict. When that conflict is going on, you are not at ease at all. So any thought that comes up, it doesn't last. If you fixate on it, it will hang around for a while, but it goes sooner or later. Even if it goes on for a week or two, it still goes.

Q: I know the answer is not in the mind, so am I conscious of the fact that I can't look there for the reason why. Why am I still conscious of the form? Are the efforts of the form just part of the greater form of everything that I am in?

Now you are conscious of the form there (as yourself). And when you look out there (the external world), are you conscious of the forms out there, too?

Q: Yes, I am conscious of the images out there. But I know that they don't exist.

So you are conscious of that thing you call 'you'. Is that an image also?

Q: That, too, is an image.

Does that exist?

Q: No, that image doesn't exist. But what I am conscious of is the density of that image. I can feel the beat of my heart, and I can feel my breath. And even though they are labels, which I have attributed to what I consider as vibrations, it is like being aware of energy or vibrations coming through, and they have different frequencies. So I interpret those frequencies to mean what they are.

If you are not interpreting them, what are they?

Q: Just energy.

They are just energy. Everything is that same energy. So what is the problem?

Q: It is like, how do you live with it without having to constantly come back?

Now wait a minute. Go back to the first thing you said. You are conscious of all these forms. You are conscious of the images as just images. What is the basis of what has gone on?

Q: It is awareness.

That consciousness or awareness or whatever label you put on it. You are still taking the position of one of the many things that are appearing in consciousness. If you took the position of consciousness itself, not as any of those images, can there be any labels? It is just patterns appearing on consciousness.

Consciousness or awareness hasn't changed. It hasn't moved or done anything. The patterns have come and gone. One finishes and another one starts. Now, as you say, is there any density in that consciousness?

Q: When I look out, there is no density. But what I feel within, I guess it is like ...

Where are you judging the 'without' and the 'within' from?

Q: From the reference point 'me'.

And what is that?

Q: It is another idea.

So what is it?

Q: It is an idea that has a vibrational energy.

Has the idea got the vibrational energy or is the vibrational energy causing the form, shape or pattern of an idea?

Q: The latter.

If you weren't conscious and aware, there couldn't be an awareness of either of them, or a name.

Q: No.

So, take that which you are taking to be real to be only appearance, also. Now where does consciousness start? Can you put a reference point in that consciousness?

Q: No you can't, because it just is.

They say that it is one-without-a-second. All there is, is consciousness or awareness. So, if you can't put a reference point in it, and it 'just is', That is you! Now, is there an inside to it? No inner and no outer. Can you grasp it with an idea or an image?

Q: No. I guess that is what I have been trying to do. Then I go back mentally and say that there is nothing to grasp.

Just see that it is 'no thing' to the mind. It can't latch onto it or put a label on it. But can you negate that, that is-ness, that consciousness?

Can you drop all ideas, all thoughts, all feelings, the whole lot in the moment? Just do it. Do you fall apart if you do that? What is left, what remains? To use words, we call it awareness–presence. Now is there any centre to it? Some place which you can say it is 'here'?

Q: No.

So 'here' is everywhere. Relax in that. Are thoughts still coming up?

Q: Yes.

Still hearing the cars, seeing the shapes and forms?

Q: Yes.

Still feeling the heartbeat and the densities?

Q: Yes.

And what are they? All appearances. All appearing on that which is 'no thing'. You can't name it but we call it 'no thing'. It is the unlimited potential that everything appears in and on. So, look around and see that everything is cognised. You see the empty space and you see shapes and forms. There is no going backwards and forwards. But where you believe there is density and heartbeats, all the shapes and forms and appearances and possibilities, in this seeming going back and forth or higher or lower, have you ever moved out of consciousness?

Q: No.

Can you?

Q: No.

If we are talking about one-without-a-second, then you must realise that that is what you must be. Who I really am! Because it hasn't changed. It hasn't got any shape or form. The sword can't cut it. Water can't drown it. And the wind can't dry it. Fire can't burn it. It is not happy or sad.

Q: The mind comes in and says I don't really exist. But I think the problem is that I don't truly believe it.

You are existence itself. Pure existence. There is no centre or reference point there. Consciousness is existence itself, on which everything appears and disappears. You can't negate that.

Q: I thought the message was to keep denying the presence of 'you'.

No. All there is to this investigation is to have a look and see if there is a 'me' or 'you' there. It is not a matter of denying it. It is seeing it for what it is. It is only a mental image or picture based on past events and experiences. 'I am so and so', 'This is what has happened to me', 'I have done this and that', 'I don't like cats', or whatever it might be. That is the mental image that you refer to or the centre that you believe yourself to be. Investigate that. See that it is only an image based on the past. It is a dead image. In seeing that, you don't have to constantly keep doing it.

Investigate until you really see that there is nothing there, until you see that it has no independent nature and no substance. In seeing that, you can't believe it anymore. You need to look at this until you see that there is nothing to which I can say 'This is what I am.' Then you must realise that you are that 'no thing-ness'. Or call it consciousness or awareness. It does not matter what you call it. The label is not it. You will never be able to grasp it with a label/or concept. It is non-conceptual awareness. That doesn't mean you have to chop off every concept either.

Look at it literally. If you don't understand what a concept is, then look it up in the dictionary and get the meaning of it. See that everything, every label, is a concept. The concept is not the actual thing. You can't drink the word 'water'.

So then, even though concepts are going on, understand that they are going on in that awareness. None of those concepts are attached to that in any way, shape or form. None has any independent existence and none can appear outside of that. So you must be that non-conceptual consciousness or awareness.

Got it?

Q: *Yes, I've got it now.*

(To someone else) Have you got it?

Q: *I think that we know it but the mind says, 'I don't know it'.*

Well, have a look at that. Could the mind say 'I don't know it' if there wasn't that intelligence–energy vibration appearing as that thought 'I don't know it'? It is a subtle trap. Whichever shape or form, appearance or possibility that it vibrates as, it is still only that. There is a knowing there, that the idea 'I don't know it' is appearing on. You are that knowingness. Knowingness itself is pure intelligence.
(*Long pause*)

Q: You know last night I listened to the CD, and in particular track 10 that has more relevance for me. I don't know why. You are talking about experiencing and the experiencer. Especially at night I do this visualisation, like, 'OK. This person here is just an illusion or thoughts, and I can let myself drift off. Then I think, 'Hold on, that is just an experience, too'. My mind is quickly jumping back and forth. I have to allow that to be because I don't have the time to be able to stop it.

Good! That is the experiencing. These things are happening in the experiencing. When you try to stop one or go along with one, you think you are the experiencer.

Q: I keep imagining that I am this big screen that I am a part of. Then I can justify …

There are no parts.

Q: No, I know. But I can then say I am one-without-a-second. It is not me that is being lived. It is this play that is being lived. I can easily go with that. But it's like there is this energy fault that pushes that 'anger button' or the 'foul mood' button. I feel uncomfortable.

If the so-called 'foul mood' comes up, and there is awareness of that, it is just what is. But when there is a label that it is a 'foul mood', it becomes an experience. Even the label is what is. But when it is believed in as 'I have got a foul mood', who has the foul mood? If it is just what is—unaltered, unmodified and uncorrected—if it is left at that, when the label comes up 'this is a foul mood', leave that also just as is—unaltered, unmodified, uncorrected—as what is. Then the next idea that comes up, 'I shouldn't be like this', which comes up from the habit pattern, leave that also. Realise that there is no one to take a stand anywhere. Then watch it all flow. As soon as you go with the idea 'I should be like this', there is a resistance to it. If you don't like it, you want to change it (alter, modify or correct it).

Have no reference point anywhere. Reference points will come up just like beliefs, labels and choices. But there is no choice maker. There is no one to have the beliefs. Leave everything flowing. A thought will come about choice: 'I will do such and such'. Then another thought appears in consciousness: 'No, I won't, I'll do this'. Then something completely different happens and the thought comes up: 'Oh, I chose to do that'. Who is the 'I' that chose to do it? There is no 'I' as such. There is no mental image there with any substance or independent nature able to do anything. It just gets done. It is a marvellous display in all its diversity. So many things are going on.

Q: So there is no rhyme or reason to it?

No. All the diversity is working away there: the germs and microbes, our thoughts and emotions, the sunsets, the clouds, the grass growing. Think of the myriad of differences in the diversity of that display. Marvel at that diversity of that intelligence–energy. All appear and disappear in that. It appears in so many shapes and forms, but it still hasn't changed in its true nature or essence. It has formed that pattern (you) to experience that which you call 'you'. The pattern got caught up in the conditioning and the belief that it was a separate entity. So it suffers accordingly. Then something brings it along to this, and something is pointed back to its own true nature.

Q: Why isn't there relief in what you are telling me? I know that there is freedom. It is freedom. But it is as though there is an acceptance of what you are saying as being true, but with it comes absolute terror as well. I know that I have never been in control because I can see that. It is as though I am an ant, and I am going to get squashed by this torrent of life.

But what is getting squashed? The pattern.

Q: That is part of it as well, I suppose.

Yes, so why the terror?

Q: Because the pattern is feeling that it is out of control.

Yes, that is the habit pattern, the belief that you are the doer. The belief is that if you let that go you will get squashed or you can't go on living. Go into it and have a really good look at it. Realise that from the sperm and the ovum, when there was no pattern that you call 'you', that intelligence–energy was in those two things, two patterns called 'sperm' and 'ovum'. And it allowed it to double and re-double and grow. It grew that body. Where was the terror then? Where was the concern about whether you would even reach the stage that you would even be born? When you came out of the womb and took your first breath, was there any terror then?

What I am getting at is that it has brought you to this point. If you realise that, why would there be any concern about letting go? Let it take you to where it is going to take you. That genetic pattern that you are so concerned about may fall into place and function very well.

Q: Can you have a functioning memory with a mind?

What we call the 'mind' is the thinking process. But there is no thinker in it. It is all just happening from that pure intelligence. Is there a thinker?

Q: Apparently, there isn't.

Well, have a look and see. Don't take my word for it. The thinker is the thought 'I think', isn't it? If that thought 'I think' is not there, and the thinking this and that is not there, what is happening?

Q: I am not sure. It is just conceptual.

Just thinking, thought, is coming up, isn't it? What we call thinking is coming up on that awareness, just the same as you are seeing right now. Before you say 'I see', the seeing is happening. So the thought 'I see' is just translating the seeing.

That is the purpose of the so-called mind: to translate what is appearing and disappearing. It is just another appearance itself. And it disappears itself, also, the same as those thoughts. Thoughts are a subtle stage of energy. What is spoken is less subtle. Words are vibrations, and it all is a movement of energy.

Q: So all that is appearing is that awareness?

Yes. And if it is understood and seen as that, are you going to get involved too much in what it is appearing as? Naturally, there is a movement, a functioning, going on. But knowing that it is only that, is it going to be a big deal? Just the same as waking from the dream: Is it a big deal anymore? Naturally, you still get caught in what the mind is telling you for a while, but you can't invest it with any independent nature or substance. So it won't last.

Q: I remember that you asked me a long time ago, in terms of feeling isolated, whether I could isolate myself from the air I breathe. At the time I thought, 'Well, what has that got to do with it?' But I see its relevance now.

The hearing of these things resonates, and they do come up when necessary. You can't possibly be separate. You can't get away from it—ever. There is no time in which you get away from it. There is nowhere to get to. It is timeless. 'I had it the other day, and I lost it'—such statements are laughable. In seeing that, and knowing that, you see the big joke of it all. It is like a fish going around looking for water.

Chapter 9
Simply Know That You Are

The crux of the whole matter is seeing who it is that gets caught up in life. What we point out here is that this is non-existent. All is only imagined, a conceptual image we have about ourselves. It's the self-bondage; that is the problem. The cause of it all is that self-centre. If we really look at, it we see that it never ever really existed. All it is, is an image we have of ourselves, based on past events and experiences and what we have been conditioned to by our parents, society, school and nation, and whatever. From all that, we form a picture of ourselves and believe that we have low self-esteem or 'I am not good enough' or 'I am having a bad time' or 'Poor me' or whatever. It all relates to that image we believe ourselves to be. Everything becomes relative to that reference point from then on. It is from that reference point that everything is judged to be good or bad, painful or pleasant, or happy or sad. So that is what has to be investigated. Who is this 'I' that thinks it has the problem?

We start here with the only reality that you're absolutely certain of, and that is the fact of your own being. Under no circumstances can you say that 'I am not'. You continually know that you are. There is no need to go around saying 'I am, I am'. That innate, intrinsic knowing is constantly with you. But then it gets seemingly obscured with all the thoughts and everything that comes up and appears on that knowingness. To translate that knowingness into words you have to say 'I am'. Yet you know that you are, without having to think about it. That is where the 'I am' thought was born. It is the knowingness or sense of presence expressing itself through the mind.

It is hard for the mind to latch onto the 'I am' thought on its own. All that the mind can do is latch onto other thoughts and concepts from the conditioning, experiences and events from the past. It becomes 'I am this person who has done this and that', 'I am no good', 'I am bad', 'I am unhappy', or whatever. See clearly that all these are just images. By constantly referring to them they become a reference point. Just imagine for a moment what would happen if you didn't have a reference point. What could you say?

Q: I suppose that it is just being.

Yes, you still couldn't negate your beingness. But without a reference point, you couldn't say it was good or bad, pleasant or painful. You couldn't say anything about it! You would just be that pure beingness, which you are always. So you see, it is imperative that you investigate and see that that reference point has never had any existence whatsoever. Who is it when you say 'I am'? Where do you think this 'I am' is?

Q: It's my awareness. It feels like my awareness.

When you say 'my' awareness, who is aware?

Q: Yes, I see. What makes it mine? (Pause) *The experience comes through a being, doesn't it?*

That awareness that you are—seemingly experiences happen in that awareness. Now, can there really be anything other than awareness? To try to describe it, the ancients use the metaphor 'space-like awareness'. It is similar to space. What can you say about space? Can you define it?

Q: No.

Has it got any shape?

Q: No.

Any form? Any dimension?

Q: *Not unless I attach it to something.*

So you see, it has no shape, no form, and no dimension. Does it have a centre?

Q: *No.*

If it has no centre, then it can't have a circumference either. All you can say about it really is that it *just is*. It just is. Now, using that metaphor 'space-like awareness', if you look at it closely, you will see that everything—this Earth as we know it, the sun, the stars all the galaxies, comets and meteors, black holes, and whatever you can conceptualise—must take place in the space. There is nothing you can postulate or think about outside of space. Is there?

Q: *No.*

If you say that there is an end to space, what would it be contained in? Space! Everything appears in space. And to us that space is no thing. It is nothing. Now, can something come from nothing?

Q: *I haven't got a clue.* (Pause) *No.*

No. So, all this manifestation is really nothing. It is really only that space-like awareness vibrating into patterns, shapes and forms. But its essence is still that space. This body, for instance, if it was broken down and pounded into powder, and then the wind came along and blew the powder away, would it be a body anymore?

Q: *No.*

Could you make it into a body?

Q: Probably not.

Every particle and subatomic particle would be in space, wouldn't it? It would all be there in space, but it wouldn't be in the shape and form that it is in now. The same with this globe that we know as Earth. If it blew up tomorrow, every particle of it would still be in space. Nothing can ever be added to it, and nothing can be lost. The patterns and shapes and forms that appear here would break down, but that space-like awareness is all that you really are. That is not limited to some particular shape or form.

Q: So you are saying that awareness is always there.

Always. The Buddhists call it unborn. 'Unborn' means un-originated. That means it has no origin. It has no beginning. It is beginningless and endless. It is timeless. It is spaceless. It is bodiless. It is mind-less. It is 'no thing'. Yet it is the essence in which everything appears and disappears. That is what you really are.

So, you see, that removes the limits we put upon ourselves. Then you can see that the labels that we put upon ourselves, the words, are the limiting factor. You call yourself a 'human being', and you call God the 'supreme being'. Take away the label 'supreme', take away the label 'human', what is left? Being. Without the label, can you separate that beingness?

Q: No.

No. That is being a chair (*pointing at the chair*). That is being a carpet. That is being the wall. Take all the labels off and what is it?

Q: Just beingness.

That's right, being. That is all it is.

Q: Yes.

Full stop!

Q: Just like that?

You see, we immediately want to rush into thought because, to the mind, that awareness is 'no thing'. The mind is full of sensations and reasoning and 'this', 'that' and the 'other'. It is a wonderful display of thoughts, feelings and emotions. But cut all that away. That awareness, to the mind, is no thing. It is ungraspable. But it is clear; it is empty; it is lucid; and it is pulsating through you right now as that livingness.

Q: But all of us are experiencing that awareness …

You are that awareness.

Q: Yes, and thought comes and goes, like what we are thinking and talking about here. None of it at the moment is being referred to the self-centre necessarily, but thought still happens.

Yes, of course, everything is still being registered: the cars going by, the movements in the room. It is all still functioning. Simply bring the focus back. You are that awareness. Instead of focusing out there on what is appearing on the mind, which we are conditioned to do, just come back to what you really are. Come back to that awareness that is 'no thing' and expand that. And you realise that it is space-like, using the metaphor 'space-like awareness'. Just like the space that encompasses the car that just passed by, does the sound come to you or does the space enclose it?

Looking from this space-like awareness, you can't even see a head or ears, so where is the place that the sound comes to you?

Q: No, that's right.

But the hearing is happening. And you realise that the vastness of space encompasses it all. The vastness of awareness is encompassing all those sounds, not out there or in here; just a pure hearing, a pure functioning.

Q: How is it that one is not satisfied with that?

Because it is very subtle. We are used to the sensations. We continue to look out there for bigger and better sensations. Or we imagine a big bang or some such thing with enlightenment or realisation. 'In the future I'll get it' or 'Oh! Won't it be wonderful!' and all sorts of imaginings about what it will be like. That is what we continue to look for. So, stay with the subtleness of it.

As Nisargadatta says, 'My silence sings; my emptiness is full'. And it does. You feel it vibrating and pulsating through you, very subtly. There is a sense of joy. It is not a highly emotional state or something that will burn you out. Stay with the subtle vibrancy. You will start to know what it is like.

Nothing can toss you from there. Nothing can touch you. Just be confident in knowing that nothing can ever toss you away from that essence that you are. Whatever is appearing—thoughts, emotions, dramas of this sort or that—nothing can ever push you away from your essence. Nothing can ever be added to it, nothing can be taken away from it. In knowing that, just allow that confidence to grow.

Without any sense of person, just being, drop all ideas of 'I'. What can you say about it, without going into your mind?

Q: Yes, well, I can't say anything about it.

You can't say anything without a thought. But you're hearing?

Q: Oh, yes!

You're seeing?

Q: Yes.

So the functioning is still happening without any mental image. There is an awareness or a sense of presence there.

Q: Yes.

What do you need to do to acquire that?

Q: Ah! Well you don't need to acquire it.

It is there of itself, self-arising, self-knowing, timelessly and ceaselessly. Again, without a thought, what conditioning is there? Where is your conditioning, without a thought?

Q: Yes, that's right. There isn't any.

Right. People try to analyse and get rid of their conditioning. The only way to get rid of your conditioning is: full stop! Right here, right now, without thinking about it, there is no conditioning whatsoever! In the next instance there may be so-called conditioned responses, but if they are not related to 'my conditioning', then the activity will take place.

The title of this book is *What's Wrong with Right Now? (Unless You Think About It)*. To do that you have to pull up and stop thought, even if it is only for an instant. Then you realise there is not a thing you can say about it. But you can't deny the fact that it is as it is. As it is, you can't say that it is good, bad, pleasant, etc. It is just what is. What *is* means it is unaltered, unmodified, uncorrected.

It is like a camera taking a photograph of everything in this room, just as it is. The camera does not say 'I don't want that object' or 'I'll have that bit in because it is more pleasant than the other'. It is just taking it just as it is. And this is precisely what is happening in the functioning with you right now. Then it is referred to the 'me' of memory. From there it is altered, modified or corrected with some preference, partiality or comparison. And all problems arise from that.

It does not mean to say that these things will not go on. But if they go on, they are understood. You have to see this clearly and understand it. And, in the understanding of it, let it go. Then there is no longer anyone or anything to be bound by it. Where before, in believing it, there is that bondage to it. That is the bondage of self. That is our conflict, the resistance to what is.

Chapter 10
Realise That

Well, you have all been here before. What questions do you want to ask or what do you want to discuss?

(Long pause. No one has any questions.)

All right, no one is saying anything. In that space, that silence, there is an awareness. The sounds, the seeing and the thinking are going on. It is just ordinary awareness or wakefulness. You're awake. There is no use in trying to grab it with the mind, because you can't. Realise that thoughts are coming up on that awareness, just like the sound of the cars is coming into it and disappearing in it. We use the metaphor 'space-like awareness'. Just see the space in front of you and the activities there. Can you move away from space? Can you part the space or chop it up? Realise that awareness is exactly similar to that. You can't move away from it or into it. Being one-without-a-second, it contains even the space. That is what you are.

Now, does it have any beginning with you, or you, or you, or me? Imagine twenty billion light years out there in space. Is it any different from the space that is here? If you are not using a specific reference point (yourself), is there any duration to it? Time is only duration. Space is volume. So they are really one and the same thing. To get from there to over there it takes time. If there is no 'me' and there is no 'there', I am already there, everywhere.

Realise that this (your body) is appearance on or in awareness also, isn't it? You see, then there is the crossing of the street or whatever, but you're not taking that as a separate entity. You're still functioning as that particular pattern of energy (yourself). If it is just that pure awareness, it can't know itself. It can't express itself. It is just unity. Just like space: space can't see itself or know itself.

So, what happens is that a pattern forms as that body–mind that you call 'you'. It is just a pattern of energy, seemingly enclosed. But what is the first thing you are seeing? Space or emptiness. So, space can't see itself. However, through this pattern it sees itself. It knows itself. Remember that we are using the metaphor 'space-like awareness'. So it is awareness that sees itself and knows itself.

All this manifestation is patterns, different patterns seeing patterns. It is only awareness expressing itself as patterns. It may be called 'different things', but in reality it is still only the display of awareness.

Q: So, this self-knowing awareness doesn't have any preferences. To it, it doesn't matter what happens.

No. Because what could it have preference for? It can only know itself. So it knows itself as awareness only. There is not a pattern there. It can't divide; space can't divide itself. There is nothing to know or no one to know.

Q: In the spiritual tradition there is this desire that arises in the seeker to know oneself. How is that related to this?

The desire to know oneself is the trying to find some reality to this pattern. When it realises that it can't find it in the mind or in the pattern, then it really turns back on itself.

Q: And it doesn't find anything.

No, because it never left what it was.

Q: I understand that it manifests itself as different patterns and that it doesn't have preferences; that it only knows itself, that you can't grasp it with the mind. But something is missing.

But you can see it. What is that body made up of?

Q: Skin and bones.

Yes, and what are they made of? Go right into it.

Q: Well, atoms?

Yes, sub-atomic particles, elements. They can be broken down to nothing. So it seems to be a solid body. But in between those minute particles is space. They are floating in space. There is space all around them and space inside them also. It seemingly forms a solid thing. Have a look at your mind in the same way. What is your mind?

Q: So you can break it down to the same thing, energy.

Energy! So you see it hasn't really changed. You can dissolve the pattern if you look at it closely. The body and the mind dissolve, and what are you left with? You can dissolve all the mental images you have about yourself by looking closely at them, by seeing the falseness of them. But you cannot negate your beingness. Even with that image of a body–mind, you cannot say 'I am not'.

Q: So you say that everything is energy. So what drives it, what powers it?

Well, energy itself is power, isn't it? What is electricity? Show me electricity. What powers that light (*pointing to the overhead lamp*)?

Q: Electricity.

What is electricity?

Q: Energy. Where is the source of the energy you are speaking of?

Where is the source of the electricity that powers this light? Where is the start of that?

Q: Oh, there is combustion, and you can actually pinpoint a source.

Can you? (*Everyone laughs softly*)

Q: Turbine!

Where does it start?

Q: (Laughing) I don't know, that is why I am asking you.

(General good humour)

It is all there is: intelligence–energy. It is everywhere and every when (all the time). You only need a little friction in the sky and you'll get lightning. All the power is there. The lightning is manifesting, but the energy is there already.

Q: All right. You call it 'intelligence–energy'. From where does the intelligence derive?

That is the intelligence of knowing. Now, when you say 'where', that implies a starting point to it. Where is the centre in space? Is there one?

Q: I don't know. I have read books that say the universe is expanding.

Where is it expanding from? Where is the source of it?

Q: I suppose what I'm asking is: do you think that there is some creative force that is driving all this energy in the universe?

The energy itself is the force. It is intelligence–energy. It keeps all the planetary bodies in orbit. It is growing this body right now. It is intelligence–energy that is in the sea.

Q: But when you say ' intelligence–energy', I think that there must be something that created that intelligence–energy.

It is uncreated. No origination. It is ceaselessly arising. It is 'no thing'.

Q: So you don't think there was the Big Bang?

There could have been, but that would be what? It can only be just another appearance on it, just the same as the whole manifestation is appearance only. It still has not changed its true nature.

Q: I think what limits us in understanding this bit is how we see things. If our eyes were like electron-microscopes and we could look at the minute level at everything, then there would be nothing there—except energy. Then I would understand that this hand is just empty space. The eye can only see superficially—the surface. But at that deeper level the energy becomes apparent. This energy is what you are calling awareness—is that right? And the energy appears in patterns.

Yes, and the patterns are only that in reality. Our eyes can't see at that level. It is hard for us to see that the image that we have about ourselves is not the real thing. Just like the microscope reveals something, through seeing, by looking into this image of what we believe ourselves to be, we see that it is not real.

Q: But we are taught that the mind is the intelligence.

Yes, you are conditioned to that.

Q: Just like, the more you learn and store away, the more power and success you will have. Everything is based on that. This is like 'me' being deconstructed of all of that. The mind is like a robot in a sense. Is it just habit patterns? Is it anything other than that?

Well, it goes along with the habit patterns. It is a wonderfully creative instrument. The problem is that we are trying to grasp it with something that has no power at all. The mind itself has not got the power. The 'I' thought can't see, can't hear, can't be aware. So it is trying to get the power and be the power, but it can't. Realise that you are the power itself that has formed that pattern of energy (yourself) and continues to form it and keep it in that pattern. It is living you as you. Get this mental image, which is putting the boundaries on it, out of the way. Then there is freedom from all that limitation that we put upon ourselves. Now, because that limitation is energy also, energy goes into that and gives it a seeming sense of reality.

Q: That is what it seems like to me. In reference to me, it is just a whole lot of habits. There are a whole lot of pre-programmed responses to a particular event. It is just like going from one to another.

That is why I say at the start, 'Sit with that ordinary wakefulness'. It is there; it is immediate; it is there with you right now, without any conceptualisation on it. It is just pure ordinary, commonplace, everyday awareness. What happens is that we try to grasp it with the mind instead of simply sitting with it.

Realisation starts to form as a knowing that everything happens in awareness. Any responses will happen by themselves. It is effortless, just like breathing, digestion, and even thinking. But the conditioning comes up that 'I am thinking this'. In that we have created a 'thinker', which we believe to be 'me'. But that is another thought. The thought 'I am' (that has been built on with past memories, conditioning and experiences) has formed a mental pattern or picture of it, but it has not got any power whatsoever.

What you call a deconstruction is just a 'seeing through'. There are still going to be patterns of energy. There will still be thoughts. But instead of translating it from the point of view of the 'me' of past memory, the responses will come up of themselves from that intelligence. Intelligence can't do anything by itself, but the response or the urge (or whatever energy is there) is then translated by the mind.

Q: So, intelligence can't do anything of itself?

No, it is pure intelligence–energy. It never changes. It changes only seemingly so. It would not be reality if it changed. The whole manifestation appears to be in these patterns. Nothing really has ever happened.

Let's take the mirage as an example. There appears to be water in the mirage, is that right? Now can that water in the mirage wet your shoes or can you step into it? It can't do anything. Why? Because it never really existed. It only appears to be so. It never ever was water and never will be.

So it is the same with this. This vibrates into different patterns, and the mind translates it into good or bad, or this or that is going to happen, or whatever. All are thoughts, ideas or images. But that is still the same. It is still only energy.

Q: Is the intelligence–energy aware that all that it observes is not real? Is it something that it wishes to do to amuse itself?

It is just pure knowing, the activity of knowing, not knowing this or knowing that. There is a registering of everything just like the mirror reflects all that comes before it. Just like the mirror, everything just registers on that pure intelligence–energy. But in that registration there is nothing that can be done about it until it is translated by the mind. We get back to 'What's wrong with right now?, unless you think about it.'

You see, you're hearing that tram go by. You immediately know that it is a tram. Realise that that sound is registered just as it is. In that registration there is an immediate knowing it as this, that or other.

Q: I am missing something here. Is the intelligence–energy creating the sound of the car?

No.

Q: It is hearing it?

There is hearing, seeing, knowing. There is no 'It's hearing.' If it is translated as 'It's hearing it', then there is a hearer. The mind puts a label on it and divides it into a seer, a hearer or a knower.

Q: What do you mean that it did not create that sound?

Well, it doesn't! It is another appearance. It has no reality as such. It only appears to be so, just like the mirage or the blue sea. All the appearances are the display of pure aware-ness.

Q: Created by the intelligence–energy or not created?

Not created. They have no reality.

Q: As an illusion, as a play? Doesn't consciousness create every-thing?

There is nothing created. It only appears to be so. Turn around and look at the reflection in that mirror. Has the mirror created the reflection? It appears to be so, but it is still only the pure energy. You see that is still the pure mir-ror. The reflection is in it, but if you really look at it, it is not really in there. It's neither in it nor out of it. It is not touching the mirror in any way. Try to put your hand in the mirror and grasp the reflection.

Q: But without intelligence–energy it would not be there.

No, nothing would be there. Everything is that.

Q: Yes, so it does create it! We are splitting hairs here.

Do you dream at night?

Q: Yes.

How real is your dream when you wake up?

Q: Well, I can see that it is not real.

You could say that it was created, but was it created? They can all feel very real, but where are they when you wake up?

Q: Is it because there has to be duration if something is created—in the sense that this moment has no beginning and no end, it is just presence, ever-present and ever-changing? The mind creates the duration with a description of whatever is happening. That is a psychological reality. It is a process that emerges from that immediate energy but is an illusion in that the word cannot be the real, as you put it.

Yes.

Q: How come we can't see that energy?

Well, you can't see any energy. You see the expression of energy. You can't see the wind, but you see the expression of it with the movement of the trees.

Q: The appearance is an expression of the pure intelligence—energy. Is that correct?

Yes. It's just not real.

Q: So, as pure intelligence—energy, that is all it is. Is that what you mean when you say that the appearance is not real?

Yes, it has not moved away from the One. That One is 'no thing'. It has no shape, no form. It is really only awareness.

Q: Consciousness is continually moving, continually changing.

Knowing that it is continually changing with the moment, alert, watching expectantly, seeing what is unfolding next. Whether it is good or bad, pleasant or painful, just wait for it to unfold, knowing that the dream is going on.

Q: So for someone like you—something comes towards you and it is not very nice, you don't like it.

Yes, whatever is appropriate will come up. There may be certain responses to it, or whatever.

Q: But you won't have any attachment to it afterwards?

Whatever response that comes up is usually acted upon spontaneously now. There is no, 'Oh, I shouldn't be like this'. Just take note of that spontaneous action. It may be giving someone a smack in the mouth, or whatever it is.

Q: But your thoughts are still that you don't like something.

Yes, but you have known beforehand. It is not attracting that intelligence–energy before it is translated into a thought. In the immediacy everything is registered. It is cognised. Then it is translated as 'I don't like it', or whatever. And that is neither accepted nor rejected now. A further response may be added to that 'I don't like it', such as 'I should do something about it'. But if that is neither accepted nor rejected, if you are not taking a stand anywhere, you allow all these things to come up and the activity follows.

Q: You are just watching it happen to you.

Even that idea of watching it is a concept. The understanding is that I am that one-without-a-second. Whatever takes place on it, this pattern here (Bob) just goes on the way it has always gone on. There is no concern as an 'I', if you understand what I mean. From that understanding, the world is carrying on as it should. If I find myself not liking something or reacting to it, that is what is happening. If there are aches and pains in the body, then that is what is happening, too.

Q: So what part of you is not accepting or not rejecting these things?

There is no 'me' here that can accept or reject. That is the understanding. If there is accepting or rejecting happening here, then that is what is happening in the appearance also. Just the same as day or night coming onto the sky: Is there anything out there saying, 'I don't want it to be night time'? Or 'It shouldn't be winter' or 'It should be spring'?

You are just the flow or seeming flow of intelligence–energy, although there is nothing really happening as such. It is just functioning like that.

Q: Is it that you mirror back whatever is appropriate at the time? I feel as though I have an understanding of what you are saying or there is a catching of it, but then the 'me' comes out and says it's a lack of responsibility or a lack of concern for other people's feelings ...

Yes, but what I am saying is, even when that 'me' comes out, what is it happening on?

Q: On awareness.

So it is just the same. Is there any 'me' there, that can 'do' any 'thing'?

Q: No.

Even this 'lack of responsibility' idea that comes up, that is part of the play also. In other words, it is just one-without-a-second. That is what you are. It is appearing over 'here' as 'this' and appearing over 'there' as 'that'. It still hasn't changed. You are that one-without-a-second, whether there is a realisation there or not.

Testimonials

Reading this book will question and challenge what you believe to be reality, what you believe to be the truth. You will begin to see life from an entirely different perspective, one that will free you from the baggage that prevents you from living a happy and fulfilled life. May this understanding come to you as it did to me, through Bob's teaching.

David Black

I first met Bob Adamson two years ago. What first attracted me to his teachings was the one-without-a-second concept of God: omnipotence, omniscience and omnipresence. If God is everything, what room is there for this idea of a self-important entity called 'me'? Then came the understanding, that I am not my thoughts, that 'my' life is being lived. And that events are not controlled by 'my' thoughts. Thoughts themselves are an expression of this one consciousness or beingness. Another realisation came, that there is no other time than right now. All power and knowledge are available only in this moment of all-presence. The mind itself is but a tool that can only think in terms of a past or a future. It is not the controlling factor.

Bob, who has been very generous with his wisdom, has helped me to see that no matter what is going on in the appearance of life, all is fundamentally all right from the position of right now. Looking at life from the position of awareness or consciousness, rather than from the shifting reference point of 'me' or 'my' mind, has helped in making life more carefree, effortless and productive. I can now see life as a great adventure, an adventure that is happening always now.

Cliff

What I like in the talking and listening with Bob is his absolute unshakable clarity. When I first listened to Bob, I was full of anger, unhappiness and suffering. That dropped away with the realisation, as Bob pointed out, that I am awareness. He showed me that it was my mind running over old patterns of torment and creating the suffering. If we are all pure awareness, then 'all' means 'all', no exceptions—not a 'me' and 'awareness'—but one awareness.

When Bob asked me to look for myself, I saw that there is 'no thing' I can locate called 'me'. There is a collection of ideas and interpretations that I have called 'me', held in memory. But in truth there is only awareness.

If awareness is all, how can there be a 'me' or any 'other'? We are all that one awareness. Within this understanding, how can there be animosity for any perceived 'other'? If I know that there is just this awareness and nothing else, then how was there ever any separation?

Bob expresses the truth with such clarity and simplicity that there is no misunderstanding and no doubt. There is no need to understand jargon or interpret what he says. It is clear. There is nothing to do, no practice to pursue. I understand that I am awareness—now.

Jan Dobbs

The search started in childhood. I first looked at Christianity and then moved to science and logic to give me the answers in life. As an adult, my search moved to psychology and later to eastern philosophy and Buddhism. I was getting closer! By my early 50s, I was hot on the trail! It was the non-dual writings of 20th century sages. I even travelled overseas to meet some of them.

Then in '94, I met Bob. His approach was very different and very simple. 'The answer does not lie in the mind', he said to me. At other times, he would ask, 'And who is it who is asking the question?' I now smile at how furious I felt at these times.

Well, after a while at Bob's meetings, it became very clear that there is nothing to get and no one to get it. I am not that searcher and (paradoxically) never was.

Please read this book. The profound wisdom in Bob's spoken words is simple and beautifully clear. They show you that your search is futile; they show you what you are not; they show you what you are and what you have always been. And at that, you may laugh and laugh!

Col

Bob clearly and simply points back to what I am. Realising my true nature has changed my life.

Brione

Meeting Bob Adamson or reading his comments on life is nothing short of a gift. Simply and humbly, yet in no uncertain terms, he makes it perfectly clear 'who you already are' by relentlessly pointing out 'who and what you are not'.

Bob's message is not polluted by spiritual carrots and conceits. He has no need to slowly impart to you the imaginary 'something' that the mind likes to envision it might 'one day' (in the future) attain. Instead, he points with supreme conviction to the only thing or 'no thing' that cannot be negated, which is our own present awareness, 'this and nothing but this—unaltered, unmodified and uncorrected'. I highly recommend reading and listening to Bob Adamson.

With great love and appreciation for this man.

John Linland

When I came across Bob Adamson's teachings in his book and CDs, inner changes started to happen. There was not a conscious effort, but I could feel the grip of the conceptual thoughts spontaneously beginning to loosen. Things were shifting and falling away. Intuitively there was an experience of freedom, and I sensed it was right.

In 2003, I was able to visit Bob, attend his talks, and have several dialogues with him. It soon became clear that I had at last found someone with a clear and unshakeable understanding of his true nature. Bob explained that the understanding had come to him through contact with Sri Nisargadatta Maharaj in 1976. Bob was able to clarify spiritual questions and issues that I had not been able to resolve in many years of seeking. In spite of my having a pretty good understanding of the teaching of non-duality (from reading books and seeing a variety of teachers over the years), it never really came home to me completely until I met Bob. Because he was so utterly clear on all this, it enabled me to see it for myself relatively quickly. I had never had this type of experience with other contemporary teachers.

With Bob I found a penetrating clarity and energy that really worked for me. His teaching is a no-nonsense, direct pointing to the truth of our own being. Bob is one of the best-kept open secrets in the world of contemporary spirituality.

John Wheeler

Forthcoming Books from Stone Hill Foundation Publishing

Presence–Awareness: Just This and Nothing Else
Talks with "Sailor" Bob Adamson
EDITED BY JOHN WHEELER

This second volume of dialogues is a follow-up to *What's Wrong with Right Now? (Unless You Think about It)*, transcribed and edited by John Wheeler. **Bob Adamson shows how the search for enlightenment is itself the trap.** We are already what we are seeking. We have never been anything other than that, and never could be. We hear that but consider it not good enough. We will race away and look at somebody else, read another book, or do this or do that, thinking we will get the answer somewhere else. But the only place the answer can be is with us. We are already that. We can't be anything other than that **Price: Rs. 275, pages 148, size: 5 ½ x 8 ½ in. NONDUAL SPIRITUALITY**

Awakening to the Dream
LEO HARTONG

"This book is written with a clarity of perception that is rare to find in the multitude of published outpourings that these days purport to express wisdom." **TONY PARSONS**, author of *As It Is*

For most readers, the author's realizations will go against their direct experience, a certain indication that *Awakening to the Dream* contains that which is critical for their most heartfelt need. The bleak realities of life and sense of separation are no match for the outpouring of insights contained in this extremely readable book. The author's use of "to" rather than "from" in the title is of profound significance to all concerned about what "enlightenment" will mean to their lives.

Author comment: "The text of *Awakening to the Dream* does not state that improvement of personal circumstances is impossible, but that there is no separate you to do it. When improvements happen, they happen, and if this seems to include personal action and input, then that is what happens. In *Awakening to the Dream* it is said that there is no 'you' having a life, but only life appearing as everything including the pattern identified as 'you.'" "I thoroughly enjoyed this book. It could become a classic!" — **JERRY KATZ,** owner and initiator of the Website Nonduality Salon. **Price: Rs. 300, pages: 168, size: 5.5 x 8.5 in., NONDUAL SPIRITUALITY/PHILOSOPHY**

Already Awake:
Diologues in Nonduality
NATHAN GILL

In the play of life, is our role indeed ours? All the while there is the assumption that our nature is this "I," there is the attempt to deal with problems and to sort them out. And for every problem sorted, there will always be a further problem. It is only when this recognition of our true nature begins to arise that real peace of ease is revealed. All the "problems" are still there, but there is no longer identification with them.

Nathan Gill is a rare voice in contemporary spirituality. Speaking with consistent clarity, he points out that all prescriptions for escape from the drama of separation instead serve as its reinforcement. Compiled from transcripts of one-to-one dialogues and group meetings, the talks featured in this book present the essential message of nonduality in a profound yet straightforward way.

The short chapter "The Story" is unique among descriptions of a teacher's own spiritual explorations, especially to readers concerned about what seem to be their own vacillating states of clarity. Also included in the book, by way of introduction to the main text, is a revised version of the author's popular Web book, *Clarity*. **Price: Rs. 325, pages: 176, size: 5½ x 8½ in. NONDUAL SPIRITUALITY/ PHILOSOPHY**

Coming Home: An Invitation to Rediscover Our True Nature (Second Revised Edition, 2009)
JAN KERSSCHOT, M.D.
Foreword by Tony Parsons
Preface by Douglas Harding
With a New Introduction by the Author

When we awaken from the daydream of our concerns, all that is left is Awareness being aware of Itself. It is a recognition more familiar than anything else, more familiar than saying "I am." Then, says the noted Belgian author and physician, there is simply Being with what is. Seeing that at gut level is like Coming Home to the Self. This book is an invitation to Come Home to that recognition, to our true Self, and be absorbed in the natural flow of life. Those familiar with Zen Buddhism and Taoism may already have an intuition of this transparent vision but may lack easy access to it. And those who are familiar with the teachings of Vedanta and Tantra will be confirmed in their understanding of this "open secret." Thus, this book can be used as an initiation into a new way of seeing, into the recognition that there is another possibility, which simply transforms everything. When we suspend all opinion and hearsay and find out for ourselves, we may taste this essence that does not require either the religious or the philosophical. **Price: Rs. 325, pages: 176, size: 6 x 9 in. NONDUAL SPIRITUALITY / PHILOSOPHY** Coming soon from the same author: *Beingness: The Fullness Beyond States of Mind.* Is it possible we're just "mind constructs"? Seeing the conceptual nature of the daydream we usually believe in as our separate selves, and also understanding the relative value of time and causality, gives the reader of this book no way at all to escape a peaceful life.